# A
# FAMILY
# AFFAIR

# A
# FAMILY
# AFFAIR

## The Unauthorized
## Sean "Puffy" Combs Story

# Andrew Cable

BALLANTINE BOOKS • NEW YORK

This is an independent biographical work and is not authorized by Sean Combs.

A Ballantine Book
Published by The Ballantine Publishing Group
Copyright © 1998 by Andrew Cable

All rights reserved under International and Pan-American Copyright Conventions. Published in the United States by The Ballantine Publishing Group, a division of Random House, Inc., New York, and simultaneously in Canada by Random House of Canada Limited, Toronto.

Cover photo © Dana Lixenberg/Outline

http://www.randomhouse.com

Library of Congress Catalog Card Number: 98-96119

ISBN 0-345-42652-5

Manufactured in the United States of America

First Edition: July 1998

10  9  8  7  6  5  4  3  2  1

# Contents

The author gratefully acknowledges the support, wisdom, and encouragement of Chris Nickson. He would also like to thank Matt Hendrickson of *Rolling Stone*, Paul A. Bloch, David Dunton and all at the Harvey Klinger Literary Agency, and Elizabeth Zack and the fine folks at Ballantine Books. And my undying gratitude, as always, to Barbara Mitchell, my Queen of Darkness.

# Introduction

In the annals of pop music history, 1997 will undoubtedly be remembered as the Year of Puff Daddy. The music world has never generated a character as dynamic as Sean "Puffy" Combs. "I'll Be Missing You," the Puff Daddy tribute single honoring his fallen hip-hop comrade and protégé the Notorious B.I.G., was a number-one hit single in sixteen countries, dominating the charts for the entire summer. In its first week on sale, Puffy's debut album, *No Way Out*, sold a phenomenal 561,000 copies, instantly certifying it for gold-record status.

And that only accounts for his actions as a *performer*. Out of the spotlight, Puffy is constantly in demand as a producer and remixer for such top sellers as Mariah Carey, Aretha Franklin, and Boyz II Men. His own Bad Boy Entertainment label generated an estimated $150 million in 1997. FOX-TV is currently developing a variety show for him, and Hollywood motion-picture offers have begun to flood in. He is the owner of a popular Manhattan eatery, and the father of a young son, Justin.

Either as artist, writer, or producer, Sean "Puff Daddy" Combs had a hand in five number-one singles on the *Billboard* Hot 100 Singles chart in 1997. He is omnipresent on MTV, The Box, and BET. He was elected Artist of the Year by the readers of *Rolling Stone*, Best Producer by the editors of influential hip-hop periodical *The Source*, and has graced countless magazine covers.

He's accomplished all this in just twenty-seven years. How did he do it? Who helped him along the way? And just what lies ahead for the pop sensation known as Puff Daddy? These are the questions I hope to answer in *A Family Affair: The Unauthorized Sean "Puffy" Combs Story*.

Beginning with his birth in Harlem, this exciting story continues through his formative years in suburban Mount Vernon, and his education at an all-boys private high school and Washington, D.C.'s, prestigious Howard University. We'll watch as Combs returns to New York City and, under the tutelage of Andre Harrell of Uptown Records, revolutionizes the world of black pop music, launching the careers of Mary J. Blige and Jodeci, and minting the hot genre known as "hip-hop soul."

# Introduction

From there, our tale recounts his escalating success with his own Bad Boy Entertainment label. As you'll witness, his rising prominence in the hotbed of hip-hop culture didn't always make him popular with his peers, but listeners and MTV viewers couldn't get enough of his artists. Fueled by the triumphs of the Notorious B.I.G., Faith Evans, Total, Craig Mack, and the rest of the Bad Boy posse (all of whom you'll learn much more about in these pages), Sean "Puffy" Combs took hip-hop out of the underground and made it the sound of American popular music.

*A Family Affair* also examines Combs's many inspirational triumphs in the face of adversity: the early loss of his father; his dismissal from Uptown; the West Coast/East Coast rivalry that divided the hip-hop nation with violence; and the unsolved murder of his best friend, Christopher Wallace, alias the Notorious B.I.G. Puffy the innovator is also Puffy the survivor.

Thus, just when everything in his world seemed darkest—following the loss of his number-one recording artist B.I.G.—Combs's performing alter ego, Puff Daddy, took center stage and dazzled the nation with his fancy footwork, irresistible hooks, and opulent videos. Out of his greatest tragedy, he forged a renewed commitment to bringing music fans the finest entertainment he could produce. And he just keeps pushing further.

Unfortunately I was not able to interview Sean Combs for this book. And while *A Family Affair: The Unauthorized Sean "Puffy" Combs Story* was taking shape, Puffy was busy putting the finishing touches on the debut album from The Lox, guiding the unveiling of Mase's hotly anticipated *Harlem World* LP, and hitting the road with Puff Daddy and the Family for the "No Way Out" tour, the most ambitious hip-hop road show in history. No matter, his activities are well documented and widely discussed throughout the media and in music-industry circles, making his rise to the top easy to chart even if there's a tremendous amount of information to sift through!

At the close of 1997, *Rolling Stone* magazine asked Puff Daddy to reveal his rules for success. "Make God first in your life," he began. Do unto others as you would wish to have done to you. Don't believe everything you hear. Try to have a little fun along the way. "And love your mother." In the pages that follow, we'll watch the way this enterprising young talent translated such simple sentiments into a multimillion-dollar empire, forever altering the face of popular music.

Andrew Cable
February 1998

# 1

## In the Ghetto

Depending on whom you ask, the descriptions you hear of Harlem in the seventies can vary wildly from person to person. Roughly eight million people called one of the five boroughs of New York City home during that decade, and despite the know-it-all attitude that characterizes many Big Apple residents, most know the city's famous uptown neighborhood only through its reputation as a dangerous urban battleground.

Admittedly, Harlem had its share of problems at that time, especially overcrowding— almost half a million people, predominantly African-Americans, living in an area of six square miles. Many of the buildings in Harlem had been erected in the early part of the century and housed far more tenants than they were designed for. A number of these tenements were turned into rooming houses, with each room split into a different apartment, often sheltering a whole family. The conditions in such buildings were—well, less than ideal. There were also smaller houses, brownstones intended for single families (but often rented out to more), and newer apartment buildings designated as developments or housing projects.

Like all but the wealthiest denizens of New York City, the people of Harlem had to contend with smells of garbage, the constant noise of wailing sirens and traffic, and the ceaseless flow of people. But many wonderful historical events had also taken place in the community across 110th Street, which borders the top of Central Park. The Harlem Renaissance of the 1920s made international celebrities of important artists like poet Langston Hughes. The famous Cotton Club was a landmark of the Jazz Age, and today, the celebrated Apollo Theatre still hosts many of the city's greatest musical shows. And Harlem has never hurt for homegrown talent, having nurtured diverse icons from swing bandleader/composer Duke Ellington to the first commercially successful rap group, Sugarhill Gang ("Rapper's Delight").

This is the environment into which Sean Combs, the first of Melvin and Janice Combs's two children, was born in 1970. His mother had made a name for herself with her beautiful looks and poise. Now she was parlaying her attractiveness into a budding modeling career. Since like often attracts like, small wonder that she and Melvin were drawn to each other. He was a popular and well-liked guy in the neighborhood, with charisma that rivaled Janice's own. It wasn't long before they'd hooked up romantically.

According to Janice, she was introduced to Melvin at a party in the Bronx. She made no bones about the fact that he lived by the codes of the street and engaged in activities of questionable legality to make a living. But Melvin also had a playful side, and loved to dance. Janice and her friends often poked fun at him, because he was so proud of his fancy footwork and fly gear.

Young Sean's memories of his father would be few. There were flashes he could recall, affectionate gestures like his daddy tossing him in the air and catching him during his third birthday party. But these precious few were the only recollections he would have a chance to accumulate. In 1973, shortly after Janice gave birth to a second child, Melvin died. Sean was just three years old. For many years he believed his father had been killed in an auto accident. It wasn't until he was in his teens that he discovered the truth.

Childhood in Harlem had taught Sean about the realities of life on the urban streets. The Combses were the only family around who had owned a Mercedes-Benz, and as an adolescent, Sean began to observe disparities between the events—as he knew them—surrounding his father's death and stories other people told of life back in the previous decade. Sean began to suspect his father hadn't been the most conventional of breadwinners.

He went to the library and began rooting around to find the news of the day when his father died back in 1973; he soon learned that his father's death hadn't been as innocent as he'd been led to believe. There had been a fair share of ink devoted to Melvin Combs's demise at the time, for while running around on Central Park West, he'd been shot in the head.

Sean took this new knowledge of his real heritage in stride. His father had lived by the codes of the street, and died by them, too. The nature of the shadowy order in the ghettos was such that few men stayed at the top of the totem pole for long, and Sean understood that a shift in supremacy wasn't unusual. The important thing was, even though the events surrounding his father's death were different than he'd been led to believe, his dad's character wasn't. Perhaps he'd been running numbers or selling drugs to pay the bills, but people still remembered Melvin Combs as a good man. He certainly wasn't a gangster. A hustler, maybe, but one with a heart.

Until he turned twelve, Sean lived with his grandmother in one of countless government-subsidized housing developments. What with a gorgeous mother and showboating father, he'd inherited a bug for show business, and would model as a Baskin-Robbins ice-cream boy while still in his youth.

Meanwhile he was turning into a budding entrepreneur as well. Like many kids in the neighborhood, he enlisted to be a paperboy. Every kid was allowed to have only a single delivery route. Sean got a bunch of his cronies to sign up for routes of their own, then bought them out and took over so he'd be earning income from multiple routes.

But he had his scruples. A devout Catholic, he attended church regularly and became an altar boy. He thanked his grandmother for emphasizing the role of God in his life. He admired the fact that God loved everybody, and he tried to follow suit. "Whether you're Catholic, Protestant, white, black, gay, straight, [God's] going to love you [because] that's all He knows," Combs would remark years later in *Vox* magazine.

His grandmother's apartment wasn't in the roughest of neighborhoods, but Sean still learned to be tough early on. On one occasion, his grandmother sent him down to the store to buy her a pack of cigarettes. Another kid approached him and demanded that Sean turn over the money he was carrying. Thinking he was tough enough to stand his ground, Sean refused to turn over the cash and put up his dukes.

The fight didn't last long. Sean's assailant punched him in his handsome mug a few times and walked off with the prize. That day, young Combs learned a valuable lesson that would serve him well: don't get into a fight if you don't think you're going to come out on the winning side. But he also realized something essential about his own character. Despite the pummeling he'd taken, Sean didn't back down and throw in the towel. He was a born fighter, willing to take his licks for something he believed in.

He counted his mother, who successfully raised him and his younger sister without remarrying, and boxing legend Muhammad Ali as his idols. So it hardly comes as a surprise that while he continued to get into scrapes with other boys, Sean learned how to deal with them better.

One day he came home and cried to his mother that another kid had battered him and made off with his skateboard. His mother turned him around and told him he had to march back outside and retrieve his skateboard—even if it meant he had to use physical force—before he could come back into the house. She was just reinforcing an important belief Sean had already become familiar with: If you're going to be a survivor, you can't be afraid to fight for the things you hold dear.

But the resourceful preteen had also learned from earlier beatings. He didn't go back and get into a fight with his persecutor himself; he enlisted an older, bigger boy to exact justice on his behalf. Early on, he was growing to appreciate the advantages of a bustling circle of loved ones and acquaintances.

Although Janice also owned a home in the community of Mount Vernon, New York, she opted not to raise her children there. At least not immediately. Years later Sean would appreciate her decision. Janice didn't want her children to start their lives in the relative comfort of the suburbs, for growing up in Harlem would imbue them with the resilience and resourcefulness that comes from a childhood in the city. But strength wasn't the only asset young Sean would acquire on the streets of Harlem.

## The Roots of Hip-Hop

As in any significant art or cultural movement, it is impossible to narrow the origins of the music known as hip-hop down to a single person or geographic region. A number of early pioneers can rightfully stake a claim to being the inventor of the genre: Kool DJ Herc, Lovebug Starski, Grandmaster Flash, Afrika Bambaataa, and many others.

During the seventies, disco was the sound of urban America. And in New York, Pete DJ Jones was the premier disc jockey, mixing records with flawless execution, maintaining a constant beat for dancing. Meanwhile an

MC—JT Hollywood and Lovebug Starski were among the earliest—kept the crowd pumping with call-and-response chants and exhortations to have a good time.

But teenagers in poorer neighborhoods like Harlem and the South Bronx didn't have the cash and threads required to hear the likes of Pete DJ Jones spinning in pricey mid- or downtown Manhattan clubs like Justine's, McCoys, and Nell Gwynn's. So they improvised. The requirements were simple: a pair of turntables, some records, a mic, a cheap PA system. House and block parties sprang up throughout New York ghettos; power was often jacked by plugging into streetlights. A legion of neighborhood DJs and MCs were born.

Among the first to rise to prominence was a Jamaican transplant to the South Bronx who spun under the moniker Kool DJ Herc. With a set list that drew on funk, R&B, soul, and disco rarities, Herc would mix the hottest sections of several records back and forth on two or more turntables, isolating riffs and beats. His disciples were known as b-boys (short for beat boy, break boy, or Bronx boy—take your pick), and they embraced the new style of music Herc and his contemporaries were making.

Locking and popping to the DJ's disjointed beats, the b-boys had their own acrobatic style of moving on the floor: break dancing. Along with graffiti and break dancing, another essential component of the new movement was rapping; rhymed rhythmic chants dropped over the DJ's mixing and scratching. The term *hip-hop* arose from one of the earliest such rhymes: "Say hip, hop, you don't stop." Unlike the discos, which catered to an older crowd, the b-boy parties had no strict dress codes. Young devotees wore tennis shoes, jeans, mock turtlenecks, Kangols, sweatsuits. This was more than just a fad; for many, it became a way of life.

Sean Combs quickly became one such fanatic. His childhood in Harlem coincided perfectly with the emergence of hip-hop culture. He had an opportunity to see the finest acts of the day in their prime: Run-D.M.C., KRS-One (of Boogie Down Productions), LL Cool J. Here he was, just twelve years old, and staying out till the wee hours of the morning to catch groups that would make musical history. The fact that he had to sneak out to do so might have discouraged him . . . but not enough to miss out on the music.

Although the music and style would soon spread, first to the downtown art community and then on to California and beyond, the roots of hip-hop were firmly entrenched in the poorer neighborhoods of New York. In the early days the vibe was strictly underground, and information was disseminated mostly via word of mouth. Perhaps if a group had a gig coming up, some handouts with details would be printed up and distributed among friends, but more often than not, you knew about a show because you were living the life. This wasn't a casual thing for the b-boys. Hip-hop permeated the clothes they wore, the records they bought (and where), their topics of conversation—everything, 24–7.

Sean was in the thick of it, hanging out at venues like the Rooftop, the famous roller-rink-cum-after-hours hip-hop haven. "The Rooftop, that was a club uptown where everybody'd go, from the hustlers to the strugglers," explained Biz Markie in the documentary *Rhyme & Reason*.

"That shit was like one of the most incredible experiences ever," Sean told *Vibe*. Not that the scene was wholly idyllic. Already, drugs were creeping into the scene, influencing the social hierarchy.

An extremely addictive but inexpensive new drug—crack cocaine—had hit the streets. Dealers, some as young as fourteen or fifteen, would draw attention to themselves and their wares, driving around with tops down on their new Jeeps.

But Sean wasn't dealing drugs, which meant that he didn't always receive preferential treatment when it came to getting into clubs for free and without hassle. The ambitious Combs quickly figured out another way to grab people's attention: dancing. And it was at clubs like the

Rooftop where his fancy footwork began to make him stand out from the crowd.

Thanks to break dancing, violence remained a marginal concern, despite the gang activity going on in New York. Popping and locking on the cardboard provided a way for rivalries to be settled without guns or knives. In the dawning days of hip-hop, violence wasn't a big concern; setting up makeshift DJ systems, hanging out at block parties, and having fun to the music were. Murder was not part of the program, and even if there were altercations from time to time, b-boys didn't think in terms of taking a life to settle a score. "Punching somebody in the eye, maybe," said Sean in *Rolling Stone*. "But killing somebody? No."

# 2

## Movin' on Up

When Sean was twelve, Janice Combs decided to move the children to the house she owned in Mount Vernon, New York. Sean would later refer to his new home, an ethnically mixed, predominantly middle-class neighborhood just north of the Bronx, as "money-earnin' Mount Vernon" in many interviews. His mother worked several jobs (including teaching kindergarten) in order to keep the house, pay the bills, and feed and clothe Sean and his younger sister, Keisha. But they managed.

The neighborhood was very different from Harlem. Squirrels scampered across carefully manicured lawns. Parents shuttled kids in uniform to and from Little League games. The Combs's house was modest but bigger than his grandmother's apartment. "I can't say my upbringing was traumatic or anything," Sean told *Paper* magazine. Janice provided her two children with a comfortable standard of living.

## Movin' on Up

"My mother always tried to give me the best education at private schools," he added in *Jet*. Sean attended an all-boys private school, Mount St. Michael's Academy. He performed well in his academic studies and also played on the school football team. It was on the playing field that he purportedly earned his nickname, "Puffy." Because he was slight of frame, Sean would puff out his chest to appear more menacing on the grid. And of course, the young ladies were more apt to notice a guy who carried himself well.

But on other occasions, Sean would reveal that his temper had played a part in earning his nickname, too. When he was angry, Sean would huff and puff with exasperation. Silly or not, his friends dubbed him Puffy.

As he grew older Puffy continued developing ways to hustle his peers, both for attention and profit. Every day in the cafeteria, he'd pull the same scam. "I saved the money my mother gave me, and I would ask everybody for 50 cents," he told *Rolling Stone*. His friends would think they were helping him out. And they were . . . by lining his pockets! As a teenager, he also worked for a spell at an amusement park. Dissatisfied with his take-home pay, he took to working double shifts to bring in more income.

Throughout his youth, Puffy's heart remained deep in music. Growing up, he watched as rap and hip-hop crossed over from an underground phenomenon to a mass-market commodity. In 1979, while Sean was still living in Harlem, Sugarhill Gang scored the first mainstream rap hit, "Rapper's Delight." Built around a groove lifted from Chic's "Good Times," the track (which was originally released only as a commercial twelve-inch single, not a seven-inch 45, as was the standard in the days of vinyl records) reached number thirty-six on *Billboard* magazine's Hot 100 Singles chart, paving the way for other commercial artists like Kurtis Blow ("The Breaks").

By 1982, groups like Grandmaster Flash and the Furious Five began to break through with raps that were meant as more than just good-time music. "The Message" brought home the harrowing realities of inner-city turmoil with lines like "It's like a jungle sometimes," and rap entered a new era of social consciousness.

A few years later Run-D.M.C. hooked up with Aerosmith for a Top 10 remake of the rock staple "Walk This Way," followed quickly by the quintuple-platinum-selling debut *Licensed to Ill* by all-white trio Beastie Boys, featuring idiotic hits like "(You Gotta) Fight for Your Right (To Party!)." And once it became apparent to the entertainment industry that there was money to be made, rifts began to appear in the fabric of the hip-hop nation.

But Puffy still had an eye on show business

all through high school. His grace and dexterity on the dance floor soon translated into appearances in music videos, and he landed work in spots for artists including Babyface and British trio Fine Young Cannibals. "I always liked to dance," he later told *Paper*. This was what initially drew him to the world of popular entertainment. The magic of the performing arts had a powerful hold over Puffy. He didn't want a career in music solely for money or power. First and foremost he wanted to show people a good time.

Not that the music industry didn't have a certain unique allure, too. One fateful day, Puffy saw the promotional video for "Uptown's Kickin' It." In particular, he recalled one scene where record-label-executive Andre Harrell strutted into a well-appointed conference room and put his John Hancock on a stack of contracts. "I was attracted to the whole control factor involved," he added in *Paper*. Hustling and entertaining people were in Sean "Puffy" Combs's blood, so getting involved in music and parties was a logical progression.

Those skills continued to come in handy after his high-school graduation, when Puffy set off on a new adventure as a freshman at Washington, D.C.'s, Howard University. From the start, his mother had encouraged him to follow a path toward higher learning. The country's best-known academic institution for African-Americans, Howard was a natural choice. And even though Puffy had chosen to study business, Howard boasted plenty of celebrated entertainers among their alumni roster, including choreographer/director Debbie Allen (of *Fame* renown) and singer/songwriter Roberta Flack ("Killing Me Softly with His Song," "The First Time Ever I Saw Your Face"), who had attended on a musical scholarship.

Receiving an education at an all-black college opened Puffy's eyes further. Seeing such a variety of people from different cultures, from all over the country and around the globe, all assembled in one institution of higher learning, and sharing similar goals with them, made a profound impression on him.

Attending Howard also exposed him to the world outside New York. He learned about where his ancestors had come from, and about the rights generations of African-Americans before him had fought so hard to obtain. And being surrounded by other young people who shared his drive to leave their mark on the world encouraged him to push harder.

But Puffy had a difficult time sitting still for lectures or hunching over books in the library studying for grueling exams. He maintained a C-grade average, but diverted his tremendous surplus of drive and hyperactivity into a new slew of activities that raised his social prominence and honed his business savvy.

## Movin' on Up

When he contrasted the vibe at home with D.C., Puffy noticed the Howard social scene was lacking in the vitality of the New York hip-hop world. He decided to bring some original flava to the halls of higher learning. He began to throw parties—big ones. First he would rent a basement or gymnasium somewhere in the D.C. area. A DJ would be hired, and Puffy would spread the word via his expanding circle of friends. If there was any reasonably prominent rap act in town, he'd hunt them down and cajole the group to drop in, adding an A-list element to the whole affair. The result? His throw-downs became the spot to relax and unwind on the weekends.

The success of Puffy's parties was also due, in part, to his expanding consciousness of people from all walks of life. At Howard, he came in contact with young people from many different backgrounds: other states, other countries that were different from his own. He realized that different cities or even different neighborhoods had distinct vibes, and learned to tap into what made an individual scene tick. This would later play a crucial role in shaping his business career: Sean "Puffy" Combs knew how to show people a good time because he'd figured out what folks of different stripes had in common, and what to fine-tune to suit specific groups in a geographic region or age bracket.

Puffy not only sold tickets to the rap and

dance parties he threw, but reportedly also had a booming business peddling term papers as well. He'd even sell sodas or T-shirts if the price was right. On one occasion he saw a moneymaking opportunity in a big student protest. After an uprising on campus, he collected all the press clippings concerning the event from newspapers and magazines, fashioned them into a mass-produced poster, and sold them to his fellow students as mementos of the occasion.

"The thing about Puffy is that he has always been business minded," noted his longtime friend and Howard alumnus Deric Angelettie in *The Source* magazine. Although he put music first, even when he was a college student, you could hear the wheels in his head turning when he sensed there was a dollar to be made somewhere. When it came to generating greenbacks, his ingenuity was astonishing.

And the nineteen-year-old would demonstrate his dance steps in front of the cafeteria daily for anybody who would play audience. With so much energy to burn, it wasn't too surprising when, two years later, Puffy announced he was leaving the hallowed halls of Howard . . . without waiting around to finish his degree.

Puffy had been dedicated to attending classes and getting a degree when he began school, but he became impatient. His dreams were big and growing bigger, and his ambitions couldn't be curbed for four solid years. The emerging entrepreneur wanted to get into the thick of things right now, and resolved to find a way to do so. And the sooner he got cracking, the better.

# 3

## Welcome to Uptown

In 1988, Puffy got his first shot at the big time . . . thanks in part to an old neighborhood crony. Like Sean, Dwight Arrington Myers had been raised in Mount Vernon. He had been born in Jamaica, the son of Eulah Lee Myers, a nurse, and Clifford Vincent Myers, a machine technician. The family had emigrated to America when Dwight was four. In 1986, the 260-pound rapper had formed a group with two friends, performing as Heavy D & the Boyz.

By 1990, Heavy D & the Boyz had already racked up two hit albums: 1987's *Living Large* (which included a reinterpretation of the soul classic "Mr. Big Stuff") and 1989's *Big Tyme*. Heavy D was signed to a subsidiary of MCA Records known as Uptown, founded by the black-entertainment entrepreneur Andre Harrell.

The son of a nurse's aide and a supermarket

foreman, Harrell was eight years Sean Combs's senior. And he'd already seen much of the music business, from several sides. While attending high school, he met Alonzo Brown, and the two formed a rap duo named Dr. Jeckyll (Harrell) and Mr. Hyde (Brown). From the beginning, Harrell made no secret of the scope of his aspirations. "I grew up thinking wonderful things could happen," he admitted in a 1993 *Vanity Fair* profile. He firmly believed he was destined to enjoy a good life.

Later Harrell attended Lehman College to study communications and business management, with an eye toward becoming a television newscaster. But he dropped out after three years and began selling advertising airtime on radio. On weekends, Dr. Jeckyll and Mr. Hyde continued to work the rap circuit. "It was a Clark Kent/Superman thing," Alonzo Brown recalled of their weekend and weekday worlds in *Vanity Fair*. Meanwhile Harrell had become tight with rap impresario Russell "Rush" Simmons, who persuaded him to leave his radio gig and come work for Simmons's Rush Management company, where he quickly ascended to a vice presidency.

Harrell was still rapping, and in 1984 Dr. Jeckyll and Mr. Hyde released an album, *The Champagne of Rap.* But the album didn't connect with too many listeners (it sold roughly 70,000 copies), and Harrell and Simmons didn't always see eye to eye. Harrell felt the essence of rap was about paying the bills with musical skills and becoming famous. "And that was extra-ghetto in a way," Simmons remarked in *Vanity Fair*. Russell, who had grown up in the suburbs, preferred a more hard-core sound that reflected his ideal of the inner city; Harrell had grown up in just such an environment, the Bronx, and knew the realities of poverty.

"I had a concept of what I wanted to do musically, and it involved partying, socializing, having a good time," Harrell told *Black Enterprise*. He was trying to capture the feel-good aspect of an inner-city sound. In contrast, Russell's rap aesthetic leaned toward a more hard-core sound and image. So Simmons went on to become CEO of Def Jam, and in 1986, at the age of twenty-five, Harrell started his own production company, Uptown.

Curious to test the salability of Harrell's sounds, a much larger, better-established label, MCA Records, offered to corelease a single Uptown album as a one-off experiment. Harrell brought a compilation album called *Uptown Is Kickin' It* to the table. The record featured artists like Marley Marl, Finesse & Synquis, and Groove B. Chill, plus Heavy D's "Mr. Big Stuff." That track took off, and MCA decided to pick up the distribution for Heavy D & the Boyz's Uptown full-length *Living Large*. The album went gold. Next Harrell tried to bring R&B singer Al B. Sure! to MCA, but they passed;

MCA thought Harrell's area of expertise lay strictly in hip-hop-related projects. But when Warner Bros. scored with Al B. Sure! and started courting Harrell for an A&R/production deal, MCA began to take him more seriously.

Andre already had his own ideas about how to revitalize the increasingly stale R&B market. He'd become enamored of the music of artist/producer Teddy Riley, who had minted the smooth, R&B-flavored, hip-hop-soul groove that would become known as New Jack Swing. Their relationship went back several years, to the Dr. Jeckyll and Mr. Hyde days, when Riley had produced artists in the Rush Management stable. Harrell had an album in the can by the group Riley led, called Guy. An MCA executive heard it and, just to make sure MCA secured Riley's band, snapped up Harrell and Uptown— lock, stock, and barrel. The eponymously titled debut from Guy sold over a million albums in 1988 and eventually achieved double-platinum sales status.

Andre negotiated a deal for Uptown estimated at $75,000. He filled the lavishly appointed Uptown offices with a staff of young black producers and executives who appreciated his mission to tap into a musical vibe that captured the ever-changing energy of urban life, yet spoke to a wide variety of contemporary listeners. And he would soon meet a young man who understood his vision even better than perhaps he did himself.

## A Musical Rise

Heavy D arranged the first meeting between Harrell and Combs, and Puffy soon talked his way into a gig as an intern. That meant his beginnings at Uptown were less than auspicious: interns are the worker ants of the music industry, stuffing envelopes, making coffee, running phone interference, and generally tending to the tasks nobody else cares to do. Despite the tedious work and limited rewards, every year countless college students accept these unpaid or low-paying stints in exchange for college credits and a possible shot at a coveted entry-level position in the music industry upon graduation. So twice a week, Puffy would hop on the Amtrak train to Manhattan to get to his internship job. He'd hide in the bathroom to avoid the train conductor, because he couldn't afford to shell out for the cost of a fare every time.

Puffy took to his new role like a duck to water. "I just couldn't understand why more people weren't interested in the music industry," he confessed to supermodel/journalist Veronica Webb years later in *Interview* magazine when she asked him to recall those early days. Puffy was the quintessential intern, willing to do anything to get his foot in the door. But initially he was careful about how much, and what kind of, attention he attracted. Even as he began to make inroads at Uptown, he

28

attempted to keep his progress very quiet, lest he draw too much attention too quickly and find himself kicked out of the clubhouse.

Andre Harrell was taken with the enterprising young man from Harlem. In his mind, Puffy "set the standard for interns around here—the hardest-working intern ever," he said in the December 12, 1992, issue of *Billboard*. And once Puffy elected not to return to Howard, remaining instead with Uptown and his new mentor, Andre took the youth under his wing.

Perhaps he sensed they were kindred spirits. Eventually Harrell even went so far as to provide Puffy with new digs when he purchased an impressive new home in the New Jersey suburbs. He generously gave Puffy a room in this veritable new palace.

Puffy was determined not to disappoint his mentor. Admittedly, he was bashful and tentative in his dealings at first. But then it dawned on him that he wasn't going to make an impression and achieve his dreams by tiptoeing around people. He started to hustle, to get both his own name and the latest Uptown grooves buzzing in the right industry circles. Soon his promotional savvy began to outshine that of entire departments, and when Uptown's Director of A&R, Kurt Woodley, stepped down, Harrell tapped Puffy to fill his shoes.

"I've never let anyone down who was willing to take a chance on me," Puffy recalled in *Paper*. He could think of no finer gift to receive than the chance to prove himself to his mentor, and when this opportunity arose, he made extra sure that he didn't disappoint him. If that meant showing up an hour early for a morning meeting, just to be ready and to show people his dedication, then that's what he'd do. He made delivering that "little something extra" his top priority. And the hard work began to pay off, for all parties concerned. But not immediately.

In his role as head of A&R, Puffy was responsible not only for finding new artists, but for making sure the ones that were already signed were hooked up with the right material and producers, and continued to deliver the goods. In 1991, much of the label's talent roster consisted of young, untested R&B singers and burgeoning rappers: Christopher Williams, Finesse & Synquis, white rapper Lucas, baby groups like Key West and For Sure. Puffy tried to find ways to give the sound and image of all these artists just the right nuances that would call attention to them, and began to make significant ripples with artists like Jeff Redd and Father MC ("I'll Do It for You"), whose album went gold.

Combs even landed his own very first signing—Lady Kazan, the wife of producer "Hitman" Howie Tee. But then the group that would bring Puffy his first truly significant success in the music business also arrived in 1991.

## Welcome to Uptown

### The Jodeci Boys

Jodeci was an all-male vocal quartet from the cutely named hamlet of Tiny Grove, North Carolina. The group was composed of two pairs of brothers: Joel "JoJo" and Cedric "K-Ci" Hailey (who were also cousins of Blackstreet's David Hollister), and Dalvin and Donald "DeVante Swing" DeGrate. In 1990, they made a foolhardy road trip to New York City, determined to land a record deal. With no place to stay, and less than three hundred dollars among the four of them, the quartet set up shop in the lobby of MCA's offices, trying to snare somebody to listen to their demo.

They arrived in the Big Apple with three tapes, featuring twenty-nine songs. "And at first, they was not trying to hear us," DeVante told *Vibe*. Uptown A&R guru Kurt Woodley wasn't interested, claiming their offering lacked "bump." Once again, Heavy D came to the rescue. The rapper heard the foursome singing in the offices and brought them to Andre Harrell. The Uptown mogul was charmed by their smooth, soulful harmonies and snapped them up on the spot.

Puffy was astounded the first time he heard them. These boys were as young as he was and could sing circles around almost anyone he'd heard. "K-Ci was smaller than he is now," he recalled in *Vibe* a few years later. "I couldn't believe all that came out of him."

As fresh recruits, the quartet became Puffy's new charges. He introduced them to the public by pairing them with an established Uptown artist (a pattern he would repeat time and again, at Uptown and beyond), Father MC, on the tracks "Treat 'Em Like They Want to Be Treated" and "Lisa Baby." Soon the group began to appear at pivotal industry showcases. "Jodeci's combination of heavenly harmonies and homeboy style seemed a solid crowd-pleaser," *Billboard* noted after a special preview for an invited audience, where the quartet performed sans microphones, accompanied only by the piano.

Jodeci made its public debut late in the spring, with the hip-hop-infused single "Gotta Love." But Jodeci got lost amid the shuffle of similar bands flooding the charts at that point: Color Me Badd, Boyz II Men, Another Bad Creation. The single stiffed at number seventy-nine on the Hot 100 Singles chart, but managed to struggle to the mid-twenties on the R&B chart. The group's manager, Steve Lucas, worried that, while their involvement in Father MC's "Treat 'Em" single had generated significant interest, Uptown and MCA had pushed the group on the public too heavily too soon. This wasn't a typical Uptown Cinderella story, but Jodeci's initial placement, however weak, showed they might be headed for greater things.

With Puffy carefully guiding their development, they released their 1991 debut album, *Forever My Lady,* a month later. The foursome deftly melded musical elements of the past and future, combining the sweet sincerity of their singing style with bubbling urban beats. The result fused the Uptown aesthetic with New Jack Swing flawlessly. When reports started to circulate that people were buzzing about the title track, Uptown hurried to release it as a single in August. By November, both the song and the album had reached the number-one spot on the *Billboard* R&B chart. "Forever My Lady" also soared to number twenty-five on the pop chart. The album eventually hit the Top 20 of the *Billboard* 200, attaining double-platinum status (for sales in excess of two million copies).

Puffy had his first big hit on his hands. As the months of 1992 followed, so did more successful Jodeci singles. First came "Stay," which stuck close to the successful harmony/ballad formula, and later the crossover smash "Come and Talk to Me." The big boys from Tiny Grove began to give the Motown hit factory Boyz II Men some very healthy competition.

Jodeci had no significant rivals in their unique sound. "Not even Boyz II Men," Puffy would declare in *Vibe.* Boyz II Men might have enjoyed a wider appeal, but something about

Jodeci connected in a special way with black audiences, prompting Puffy to compare his boys with "straight chicken and grits. Boyz II Men is a salad and a veggie platter. But it's all good food."

And to keep female fans enthralled just a little bit more, Puffy made sure the members of Jodeci were never too bashful about posing shirtless.

## The Daddy's House Party Scene

When he wasn't engaged in making a name for himself at Uptown, Puffy was busy hosting the jam-packed party Daddy's House. The weekly joint kicked off in March of 1991 at the gigantic Red Zone, way over on the farthest reaches of West Fifty-fourth Street in Manhattan. Originally held on Wednesdays, later that summer it moved to Thursdays, in an effort to cut down on crowds; neighbors had complained, and called the cops to check out some two hundred patrons waiting in line.

Over one-thousand-plus party people showed up every week, making Daddy's House the city's premier hip-hop party. Like all of Sean's tactical maneuvers, the club's name had been carefully selected. The promoters counted on people being more respectful if they felt the vibe was more personal, like a house party, rather than that of a big, anonymous club.

"You're going to ask for a drink of water, you're going to ask to use the bathroom," Puffy told Chris Smith of *New York* magazine.

The proceedings rarely got quite that pedestrian. But by pairing modest, efficient security (including a metal detector) with inventive spinning courtesy of DJs like Clark Kent and Kid Capri, Daddy's House put a fresh, less threatening spin on the public image of hip-hop. And the folks in charge let the crowd know that was part of their mission, too.

A lot of downtown rap nights had begun to sour, due to a shortage of appropriate venues willing to incur any perceived risks and the continued presence of gang-related violence. After a young man was shot at a Nassau Coliseum rap show in December 1989, it became harder and harder for New York rap promoters to put together shows and parties, but Puffy refused to be deterred. "We're always on the mike reminding people that so many hip-hop clubs have gone down because of stupid behavior," he stated. He didn't want Daddy's House to come and go too quickly.

Working with promoter Jessica Rosenblum (who had already cut her teeth at popular New York clubs like Nell's and Bolido and later went on to run Mecca, the city's longest-running hip-hop party), Puffy pulled in A-list names every week. In the upstairs VIP lounge, notables such as Monica Lynch of Tommy Boy and Russell Simmons sipped Moët champagne and snacked on chicken wings. Meanwhile, visiting first-class rappers—including Ice Cube's female foil Yo-Yo (who had a Top 40 hit that summer with "You Can't Play with My Yo-Yo"), Boogie Down Productions' KRS-One, and Doug E. Fresh ("the human beatbox")—often dropped freestyle live performances on the crowd. Even Mike Tyson popped by to shake his groove thing.

In addition to plenty of celebrities, the crowd at Daddy's House enjoyed another distinction that set it apart from the average early-nineties hip-hop party. While similar clubs tended to attract predominantly male attendees, Puffy and Jessica's joint drew plenty of women. "[At] most hip-hop events, the ratio's 70-30, if you're lucky," Rosenblum told *New York*. "We get about 50-50."

Daddy's House blew up fast, blazing brightly, but only briefly. It was a fantastic night, packed to the rafters with people having fun and driven by the finest names—established and emerging—in hip-hop entertainment. But ultimately, maintaining the party's exceptionally high standards, added to Puffy's Uptown responsibilities, was too much, "so we just stopped doing it," he later reminisced in *Paper*.

# 4

## Basketball Blues

Nineteen ninety-one was a watershed year in the career of Sean "Puffy" Combs, what with his quick rise in the Uptown hierarchy and the success of Daddy's House. The latter triumph inspired his next flight of fancy—which, despite the best of intentions, would result in the greatest test of his abilities to date.

Drawing on their increasingly broad array of celebrity connections in the worlds of music, sports, and entertainment, Puffy and his cohorts brainstormed and came up with a charity fund-raiser that would allow them to utilize the public prominence and athletic prowess of these friends: an all-star basketball game. Targeting a health threat of ongoing concern in the black community, the promoters announced that they would turn the proceeds over to the AIDS Education Outreach Program.

The game was scheduled for December 27.

The place was the Nat Holman Gymnasium, in the Jeremiah T. Mahoney Hall at City College of New York. Among the featured players were Puffy's Mount Vernon friend and Uptown compatriot, Heavy D. In fact, the event was billed as "The Heavy D and Puff Daddy First Annual Celebrity Charity Basketball Game." Other participants scheduled to appear included Michael Bivins (of New Edition/Bell Biv Devoe), Big Daddy Kane, Phife Dog from A Tribe Called Quest, Redhead Kingpin, and members of Boyz II Men, Run-D.M.C., EPMD, the Afros, and Puffy's Uptown charges, Jodeci. MTV personalities Ed Lover and Todd T were also slated to appear.

With such a star-studded lineup and the Puff Daddy promotional machine running at full steam, plans for the event went extremely well. Too well, in fact. The day of the game, far more fans than anyone had anticipated showed up. The event drew as many as 5,000 attendees, although the gym's capacity was only 2,700. Anticipation boiled over, and the crowd, trying to squeeze through the gym's single open entrance, surged, pinning a number of helpless people against the other, locked doors.

Eight people were crushed to death by the mob of spectators; a ninth victim died later in the hospital; an additional twenty-eight people were injured. In a later report, at least one officer at the scene referred to the crowd as "animals." According to *Rolling Stone*, Puffy found himself on the ground, trying to revive fallen bodies that would never be getting back up.

The consequences facing Puffy in the aftermath of the carnage were substantial, and the media roundly denounced him for mismanaging the event. College officials claimed they had never been informed that rap stars would be involved in the game, and that the event wouldn't have been permitted if they had. The promoters had failed to ensure adequate security or provide insurance, as stipulated in Sean's contract with the college, but two different security forces—the Pinkerton Agency and the X-Men—were blamed for not being present in the lobby of Mahoney Hall to control the crowd.

The district attorney's office, a city-hall task force, and City College launched a series of investigations into the tragedy. On December 31, Puffy's legal counsel, Martin Barbus, released a statement expressing the promoter's sorrow and his assurances that he would cooperate fully with any investigations. But Barbus dropped Combs as a client almost immediately thereafter.

Puffy and Heavy D scheduled a press conference at the Plaza Hotel on January 2 to try to deal with unfair allegations and dispel false information circulating in the press. Meanwhile, to keep the media and legal interlopers at bay, Combs also engaged the services of two of the most powerful and well-known attorneys in the business: William Kunstler and Michael Warren (the latter would later represent rapper Tupac Shakur when he was charged with sexually abusing a woman in 1993).

Eventually, the dust began to settle, and blame was portioned out. The matter was now being investigated by the Manhattan District Attorney's Office, the state attorney general, the city council, and the city comptroller. On January 14, José Elique, head of security for the City University of New York (which includes City College), delivered his report on the unfortunate incident to the university. Elique placed the majority of responsibility at the feet of the college, whom he alleged had failed to examine the nature of the event properly, thus preventing them from adequately assessing, and preparing for, the number of attendees. Blessedly, this report did not hold Puff Daddy or Heavy D at fault for any loss of human lives.

But the story was far from over. Although the event had been billed as a fund-raiser, the AIDS Education Outreach Program proved to be a wholly unknown entity among AIDS service organizations. It wasn't recognized as a registered charity by City College of New York or any state or city agency. Some reports in the press claimed that the group was a division of the New York City Health Department, which cannot accept charitable funds. *The New York Times* claimed the organization didn't even exist.

This final assertion was supported by a sixty-seven-page report, prepared by Milton Mollen, deputy mayor for public safety, and issued by the New York City Mayor's Office a few days after Elique's. According to their investigation, even though the basketball game had been billed as an AIDS fund-raiser, none of the proceeds were earmarked for a specific charity. Meanwhile, proceeds from the ticket sales were missing for several days, until January 2, when $25,000 was turned over to Deputy Mayor Mollen's office.

But Combs didn't bear the full brunt of the blame. The city parceled out black marks to almost all the parties involved: campus and university officials, student government leaders, the Emergency Medical Service, and New York City police, all in addition to Puffy.

Mollen reserved his harshest words for the police, who he claimed exercised "highly questionable" judgment in the fashion in which they responded as the events took shape. He also cited student government leaders for failing to inform college officials that hip-hop superstars would be the event's big draw. In turn, officials at City University of New York and City College were taken to task for failure to observe their own security policies. Perhaps most upsetting, the Emergency Medical Service was criticized for their refusal to send an ambulance to the site in response to an anonymous phone call that insisted "people are dying." And Mollen echoed the officer who had likened the crowd to wild beasts, chastising those in attendance for displaying a lack of self-respect and "a total disregard for one's fellow men and women."

The only entity that escaped completely unscathed in the deputy mayor's report was popular radio station WRKS (Kiss-FM) New York. Although the radio station—whose logo appeared on the printed tickets—had run spots on the air advertising the event and hung promotional banners in the gymnasium, General Manager Charles Warfield denied that the station was the official sponsor of the game.

But even if the law wasn't going to crucify him further, Puffy couldn't escape the tremendous burden of his own guilt and shame. He suffered from fainting spells and severe depression; returning to work seemed an insurmountable task. "I was dead," he confessed to *Rolling Stone* a few years later. "If O.J. [Simpson] ain't killed nobody, I know how he feels."

Ultimately, Puffy turned to his faith in God for solace and strength. Even as he was curled up at home, filled with self-pity and losing weight, going on crying jags and believing everyone had turned against him, he started talking to God more and more. His belief in the Lord grew deeper and deeper, and carried him through the crisis. Others thought the young producer was ruined, but he felt that his faith in the Lord had saved him. He resolved to keep fighting for what he cared about.

Long after the basketball tragedy, Puffy would continue to put his confidence in the power of the Almighty. At the end of 1997, he told *Rolling Stone* the book that had influenced him most in life was the Bible. "The psalms are my favorite and also the Lazarus story." In the tale of Lazarus, Jesus Christ resurrects a dead man; the parallels were obvious to Puffy. He even took to wearing a Lazarus piece from a chain around his neck at times. "I've risen from the dead a couple of times, just through all this stuff I've been through, man." But just how deep the truth of those words ran would become apparent only with experience.

# 5

## What's the 411?

By 1992, the world of black entertainment was changing in a number of ways. Artists and entrepreneurs like Spike Lee, Russell Simmons, Keenen Ivory Wayans, and Wesley Snipes were beginning to play a larger role in the cultural mainstream, and new fortunes were being made. As the power behind one of the most significant suppliers of this revolution's sound, Andre Harrell was at the thick of this boom, traveling around the world in style and housing two BMWs in his garage. And he made sure to spread the wealth in his own fashion, throwing fantastic parties at his spacious home in New Jersey.

At these elite celebrations, the "Young, Black, and Fabulous" would sip Cristal, boogie down to the sounds of Kid Capri, and nosh on nouvelle soul food. It was a new thrill to savor the most attractive aspects of both the ghetto and the high life simultaneously. But while supermodel Veronica Webb swam laps in the pool and Andre nibbled on barbecued ribs, the ever-ambitious Puffy wasn't kicking back. His slender frame would dart from group to group as the young A&R director made connections and fostered friendships, all the while soaking up the atmosphere and observing what made people tick.

Sometimes he'd even extract artwork from his briefcase and show off the logo—a baby in a baseball cap—for the company he dreamed of starting someday. He planned to call his enterprise Bad Boy. But ironically, the musical triumph that was going to turn Puffy's Bad Boy dream into a formidable reality was actually a "bad" girl. And her name was Mary J. Blige.

## The Queen of Hip-Hop Soul

The second of four children, Mary J. Blige had been born in the Bronx on January 11, 1971. Shortly after her birth, her family relocated to Savannah, Georgia, where she spent her early childhood. But when Mary was just five, the Blige clan returned to New York.

They settled in Yonkers, in a tough public-housing project named the Schlobohm Houses. The tenants had nicknamed it "Slow Bomb," alluding to the impending despair that hung in the ghetto air. Still they all somehow managed to get by.

"It wasn't like everybody was starving, like Ethiopia or something," Mary explained to *Rolling Stone* years later. But plenty of parents in the projects held down jobs that paid poorly—if they could find employment at all. And just as in the Harlem of Puffy's youth, or the Bronx of Andre's, overcrowding was always an issue. Many of Mary's relations from the South, assorted aunts and uncles and cousins, took up residency in their cramped two-bedroom apartment.

Mary was a sensitive child, but her kinfolk didn't baby her. And the tiniest criticism, such as mentioning her relatively large feet, would send her into a tailspin. Her relations often berated her about posture, telling her she stooped, and needed to stand up straight and tall. Later, Mary could appreciate their motives. "They were only toughening me up," she conceded in *Rolling Stone*. It wasn't exactly a nurturing environment, but their actions brought out qualities she didn't always realize she had, making her a stronger person.

Mary and her sister LaTonya spent most of their life without a father figure around. Their mother, Cora, worked as a nurse. They didn't have much money, but as Mary remembers it, the girls also never wanted for anything. The sisters' father reportedly left the nest before they'd left Savannah, and played virtually no role in their upbringing.

But her absent father still passed on a legacy

to Mary—at least a portion of one. He played the bass guitar, performed regularly with a band, and shared his love of music with her. "He taught me how to sing my notes and gospel gave me the depth," she told *Ebony*. When life in the projects dragged her down, Mary comforted herself with the emotional riches of her mother's favorite records—classics from Gladys Knight, Al Green, Donny Hathaway, and Otis Redding.

By age seven, Mary was singing in the junior choir at the House of Prayer Pentecostal Church. She anticipated each Sunday with joy, looking forward to communing with other kids and testifying to her deepening faith in Jesus Christ.

Other parishioners who heard Mary's beautiful singing encouraged her to try to do something with her voice, to break into show business. "And I'd be like, 'What? I am living in the projects in Yonkers. What am I going to do with my voice?'" Blige later told *Newsweek*.

As she grew older Mary began to land solos in the choir. On other days, she and LaTonya could be found at house and block parties around the neighborhood, soaking up the hip-hop beats and flowing rhymes.

Over the years Mary continued to sing, if only just around the house. She would stand in front of a mirror, clasping a hairbrush in her hand, and emulate R&B stars of the day like Meli'sa Morgan. She'd be up first thing in the morning, singing away while the family tried to catch a little extra sleep. LaTonya would cry for her to shut up, but Mary wouldn't hear of it, and kept right on making a joyful noise.

But life in Schlobohm had also made Mary hard and defensive. It seemed like she was getting into fights almost daily. But she realized that if she didn't act tough, people would take advantage of her weakness, and rob or bully her. She likened the Schlobohm experience to being raised in a barrelful of crabs, crawling over each other and snapping their claws. "If you try to get out, one of the other crabs tries to pull you down," she told *Essence* readers.

The realities of ghetto life left their mark on her developing personality. "It seemed like I was always an older person," she reflected in *Ebony*. She should have been a carefree sixteen-year-old, but instead there always seemed to be one weighty concern or another preying on her young mind. By age seventeen, she'd begun to cobble together a life of her own, working various part-time jobs and doing her friends' hair in the kitchen of the family apartment. She wasn't a licensed beautician, but she made extra money coiffing her girlfriends in the projects.

Mary's whole life changed one evening when she went to a mall in White Plains with some of her friends. At a do-it-yourself recording franchise, her homies convinced her to show off her pipes on one of the karaoke-style tracks and make a tape. "Everybody else in the joint was singing these old rock songs, so I went in there and rocked Anita Baker!" she told *Essence*, laughing.

She took home the cassette she'd made, her own rendition of Baker's Top 40 hit "Caught Up in the Rapture," and played it for her mother. Cora in turn handed her daughter's star turn over to Mary's stepfather, James Dillard, who passed it along to a friend who knew R&B singer Jeff Redd. Redd, who was one of Puffy's protégés and part of the Uptown stable, heard something special in Mary's voice. Finally, the humble tape had landed on Andre Harrell's desk. The Uptown CEO, fresh from his successes with Al B. Sure!, Heavy D, and Jodeci, signed her to a recording contract.

Harrell had signed Blige, but her grooming and development was entrusted to Puffy, who became her Svengali, carefully sculpting her image and the sound of her music. "Puffy was really helpful in putting a vision in my mind of how the albums should be," Mary admitted in the October 22, 1994, issue of *Billboard*.

With her myriad influences, Mary embodied all the elements Puffy thought were essential to the perfect contemporary sound. The familiarity with old R&B and soul, and her roots in gospel, were important, but her love of hip-hop would distinguish Mary from the rest of the pack. She would sing on the beat, emulating rappers, instead of in the mellifluous style popular with female R&B singers.

With Puffy as executive producer, her debut full-length *What's the 411?* caused a popular upheaval when it was released in July of '92. The kids went wild for it, and within a month it was in the Top 10 of the *Billboard* charts. The first single, "You Remind Me," was featured in the movie *Strictly Business*. It went all the way to number one on the R&B singles charts, and crossed over to the Top 40 on the mainstream charts. Her next, "Real Love," did even better, reaching number one R&B and number seven on the pop charts.

Blige had delivered a fresh new sound, and had the poise of a diva to back up the musical goods. In *Entertainment Weekly*, Havelock Nelson awarded the album an "A" review grade. "Like male performers Guy and Jodeci, she bends her gospel-bred pipes around streetwise collages consisting of hard drumbeats, rugged rap samples, and hazy synthesizer lines. . . . Blige is a New Jill comer with her eyes on the prize."

Other critics likened her to icons including Chaka Khan (she even tackled the Rufus classic "Sweet Thing" on the album) and Aretha Franklin. Almost overnight, Mary J. Blige was the sweetheart of young black America. In the end, *What's the 411?* sold over two million copies. "Every black person done bought Mary J.'s album twice," boasted Andre in *Vanity Fair*. "That was one and a half million. The rest is white people."

"Mary was the first act born out of hip-hop who had a true sensibility for R&B melody," producer Mtume later observed in *Rolling Stone*. Soon she'd spawn a legion of imitators, from Monica to Monifah to her own backup singer Faith Evans. But there was only one Mary J. Blige, and soon she'd been crowned with her own title: "The Queen of Hip-Hop Soul."

But Puffy didn't see the sound he was pushing with Mary J. and his other Uptown charges as revolutionary; he was just giving the people what they wanted, a remedy to the ceaseless flow of too-smooth R&B singers dominating the charts. He thought the phenomenon people were calling "hip-hop soul" was inspired by just plain common sense. He'd simply paid attention to what his peers were listening to, and tried to distill the different elements into one package. It thrilled him to realize he had his senses so securely attuned to the rhythms of urban culture.

Puffy's new sound and vision, as epitomized by the artists he oversaw, encompassed every aspect of his own background: street style and culture, club energy, middle-class values, and upward mobility. With her platinum-blond tresses, Mary J. Blige embodied all of this to a tee, and her videos and photo shoots were filled with images of success—Chanel fashions, sparkling champagne, and luxurious furs—alongside the hip-hop fashions of the day.

Mary J. Blige had achieved success beyond her wildest dreams. She went out on tours with Bobby Brown, Boyz II Men, and Jodeci, and proved she could deliver the goods live. But she had never anticipated that she'd reach such dizzying heights so quickly, and felt unprepared. Unaccustomed to the spotlight, she developed a reputation for being short-tempered when the pressures of success began to build. Rumors flew that she was rude to journalists (when Veronica Webb was later sent to profile her for *Interview*, it almost ended in a brawl) and late for shows and photo shoots. But the fans loved her all the more. So Mary hid any confusion or hurt behind her omnipresent sunglasses and tried to take it all in stride.

"I always wanted to sing, but I never thought in a million years that I would be right where I am, right now," she admitted in *Ebony*. She wouldn't be the last of Puffy's protégés to utter such pronouncements.


## The Beginnings of Bad Boy

Despite his mounting successes, Puffy wasn't entirely happy. He appreciated his position at Uptown, but didn't feel that MCA had a full appreciation, or sufficient respect, for black music, and black culture in general. And he refused to be contained. Even selling millions of copies of a record didn't add up to enough for him. He wanted to make music that would become part of pop history. He dreamed of taking hip-hop culture to wider audiences, and pushing it further than anyone in the entertainment world had dared to previously.

Well aware that his young charge was champing at the proverbial bit, Andre Harrell moved Puffy up in the pecking order. In December of 1992, he promoted the twenty-two-year old to a new post: vice president of A&R and artist development. The promotion made Puffy one of the youngest A&R VPs in the history of the music industry.

But more important, Puffy would now have his very own management/production/record company that would be distributed through Uptown. The vision he'd shared at Andre's parties was coming true: Bad Boy Entertainment was a reality.

Andre told the media that the promotion was a reward for Puffy's outstanding achievements with the Mary J. Blige and Jodeci records. And the Bad Boy deal reflected Uptown's confidence in Combs's cutting-edge aesthetic. The label deal was prompted by Andre's feelings that "Bad Boy's inner-city point of view about the struggles and rebelliousness of being an inner-city teenager" would have continued resonance with mainstream listeners, Harrell told *Billboard* in an article that appeared in their December 12, 1992, issue.

Apparently, Puffy had been negotiating with the Uptown CEO since the summer to allow him to launch Bad Boy. Puffy explained to *Billboard* that Andre had emphasized that he appreciated how crucial he was to Uptown's continued growth and success. Harrell encouraged him to spell out his dreams, and the two men would try to find a way to realize them. Bad Boy was a way for Puffy to branch out while remaining an essential part of the Uptown operation. He wanted to start his own enterprise, but didn't want to have to abandon Uptown as a consequence.

In truth, just as Harrell had cinched the Uptown deal with MCA by showing that other major labels might want him, too, so Puffy had approached different companies for help launching his own enterprise. But the promotion coupled with the financial rewards of the label deal ensured his continued commitment to his current home: "I'm gonna be right, I'm gonna be loyal, and we'll try to continue the legacy of Uptown."

But the press noted that very few record executives had been able to hold a post at one label while simultaneously running an independent company like Bad Boy for long. Puffy insisted to detractors that his continued involvement in virtually every aspect of production and marketing for Uptown artists would only help him keep his priorities straight at Bad Boy.

And besides, Bad Boy was aiming for a moderately different sound than the slick but urban street-style rap and R&B Andre and Puffy had pioneered in the past few years. Apparently, Puffy felt constrained by the established Uptown formula. He had tried to make records that would always conform to the narrow guidelines of radio-station formats. The releases on Bad Boy were aimed instead at Puffy's own peers—people who had grown up with hip-hop culture over the past decade and were seeking something a little tougher and more authentic sounding.

Artists like Busta Rhymes and EPMD were attracting strong urban followings regardless of their popularity at radio stations. Puffy wanted to foster more artists in this vein. But he wasn't turning his back on the sound he'd built his reputation on, either. Artists like Mary J. Blige and Jodeci would have fit in just as well at the new Bad Boy label as they had at Uptown. That's because these performers had what Puffy felt was the essential Bad Boy attitude—one that reflected the unique challenges of growing up in an urban environment, where life could be harsh and demanding. That same dynamic translated into their live performances, where their singing was infused with the joy of putting on a show, yet underpinned with accents of anger and frustration.

At the time the formation of Bad Boy Entertainment was announced, it had only one staff member besides Puffy—General Manager Kirk Burrowes. In addition to releasing records, the company would also manage artists and producers. A few clients were already in place, including Puffy's old pal Heavy D, a new act named Jesse West & Third Eye, and Puffy's latest discovery, a little-known talent *Billboard* referred to as "Biggy Smallz."

# 6

## Who's the Man?

Nineteen ninety-three would prove to be a pivotal year for Puffy in many respects. It got off to a relatively slow (by Puffy standards) start, but two of his projects for Uptown would introduce the most important artist he would ever work with.

The first of these two crucial records was a movie soundtrack. *Who's the Man?* was a slapstick comedy directed by Ted Demme (nephew of Oscar-winning *Silence of the Lambs* director Jonathan Demme). The film starred popular MTV rap VJs Ed Lover and Doctor Dre as a pair of inept Harlem hairdressers who become police officers and wind up entangled in a battle with an evil real-estate speculator. A who's who of early-nineties black music, it featured cameos from Kris Kross, B-Real, Humpty Hump, and Queen Latifah. Supporting roles were played by rappers Cheryl "Salt" James and Ice-T, and even

Kurt Loder of *MTV News/Rolling Stone* fame popped up in a cameo.

While the movie wasn't a hit with the critics, and fell short in the laugh department, the soundtrack compiled by Puffy and company featured a title tune from House of Pain, plus many of Uptown's brightest stars: Jodeci (on "Let's Go Through the Motions"), Father MC, and Heavy D (collaborating with controversial reggae star Buju Banton). Mary J. Blige's single from the soundtrack, "You Don't Have to Worry," shot to number eleven on the R&B charts.

But the real gem was buried among the more easily identifiable treasures. At the very bottom of the artists listed on the album jacket was simply the name "Big." No "The Notorious," no upper-case spelling, just "Big." The track credited to the laconic but little-known rapper was entitled "Party and Bullshit." Both the title and part of the hook were lifted from "When the Revolution Comes," a cut by seventies black protest quartet The Last Poets. And indeed, the arrival of Biggie Smalls was going to prove revolutionary.

Biggie also popped up on Puffy's other notable project in 1993, a follow-up album of remixes from Mary J. Blige's double-platinum *What's the 411?* In addition to the new hit "You Don't Have to Worry," the record's twelve cuts featured new interpretations of various album cuts, plus some odds and ends. Always one to appreciate the strategy of attaching a rising star to an established one, Puffy had wisely featured Biggie on two of Mary's twelve-inch singles, "Real Love" and "What's the 411?" (the former track now appeared on the new album).

But while critics had welcomed Blige's debut album with enthusiasm, and would soon take up the cause of the Notorious B.I.G., they called Puffy out on the carpet for this album of what they felt were so-so reinterpretations. *Entertainment Weekly* complained that by removing essential components from songs, like the rambunctious piano riff from "Real Love," Puffy and company had bled the life out of many of the original versions.

*Entertainment Weekly* writer David Thigpen felt that Puffy and his producer pals had made multiple mistakes in their attempts to deliver fresh interpretations of tracks from the album that had become an instant classic and set a new standard for urban pop music. Still, the remix collection had certain merits. "Puffy's pumped-up remake of 'Love No Limit' nearly makes up for the lapses, and Teddy Riley's 'Changes I've Been Going Through' trumps the original," he conceded.

Still, Biggie Smalls, a.k.a. the Notorious B.I.G., was the emerging rap star that Puffy had showcased on these two marginal records. Smalls shared much in common with the young A&R hotshot and producer—but a middle-class background wasn't one of those things.

## The Beginnings of Biggie

Smalls's real name was Christopher Wallace. He was born to Jamaican parents, in the Bedford-Stuyvesant neighborhood of Brooklyn, on May 21, 1972. Like Puffy, he had grown up without a father figure. His own dad had split when Christopher was around the age of two—too young even to recall the shadowy man. His father returned to visit only once, four years after splitting, when his son was six years old.

His mother, Voletta Wallace, was an early-education schoolteacher. She was also a devout Christian. Biggie would later complain in the press that his upbringing was too strict. But she obviously looked out for her only son's welfare. As a child, when Biggie broke his foot falling off a public bus, Voletta took the city to court. She won a settlement of $90,000 dollars, which she saved for his future.

At times Wallace would paint his childhood as being bleak and marked by poverty. But in a *Spin* interview with writer Sia Michel, Mrs. Wallace begged to differ. She disputed the myth that Biggie was "some hooligan from a single-parent household in a run-down ghetto walk-up." She pointed out that single-parent

homes have fostered plenty of bright, prosperous children. And whatever their financial
situation, the Wallaces' apartment was always
a showplace.

One thing was certain, though. The absence
of a strong male presence in his home had
certain consequences. His mother was reluc-
tant to be blunt with him about delicate
matters such as sex education. Biggie later
told Robert Marriott in *Ego Trip* magazine
that while Voletta had told him about the
birds and the bees, she hadn't gotten much
more graphic than . . . birds and bees. Biggie
wanted to know about the nitty-gritty details
he heard whispered among older boys on
the streets. But as a schoolteacher, Mrs. Wallace was prone to taking a more academic
approach to such topics. Her son didn't dig
that at all.

Like Puffy at Mount St. Michael's, young
Christopher attended a private Catholic institution. His grades were good enough to land
him a spot on the honor roll. From an early
age he displayed an interest in art. He even
considered a career as a graphic designer. But
the impoverished quality of life in Bed-Stuy
didn't encourage such lofty dreams, and as
much as Biggie's mother pushed him toward
formal education, he was more interested in
building up his "street smarts" and being a
player.

Biggie could appreciate that his mother's

own upbringing in Jamaica had been much stricter than his, and that Mrs. Wallace had her hands full holding down a job and providing for her family. This didn't leave her with much free time in which to keep tabs on his activities, and Biggie's curiosity couldn't be curbed. He told Marriott that he wanted to find out what life was all about on the streets, and his mother wasn't exactly the best source of information; she hadn't even been raised in Brooklyn.

Every time he walked out the front door, Biggie saw that the dealers were the most prosperous players in the neighborhood. "Everything was happening on that strip of Fulton Street," he reminisced in *Interview*. If he wanted to get a pizza, or go to the convenience store, he had to do so on Fulton Street. He was savvy enough to realize that the men in fly bubble jackets, sporting high-priced wristwatches, weren't purchasing their gear with legit activities. Then he saw a story about the crack epidemic on the news and put two and two together. He knew now where the boys on Fulton Street got their dough.

Prior to that revelation, Biggie had been lining his pockets by means of other illegal activities, like purse snatching or mugging people who were drawing money out of automated-teller bank machines. But he still had to exercise discretion at home. He couldn't let his mother find out how he'd drummed up so much money, so he had to be discreet about how he spent it. He couldn't bring new clothes into the house without being able to explain them, so he actually ended up hiding his clothes on the roof. Eventually, a neighbor suggested he invest the money into a business scheme. Biggie took one look at his neighbor's expensive rings and sneakers and training suits, and the proposition sounded too good to resist.

Pretty soon Biggie was running with gangs, dealing crack and guns. He'd rise early in the morning to work his beat on Fulton Street, after hanging around the check-cashing place. He later confessed to writer Havelock Nelson, "The crackheads get checks from Social Security, and ... welfare checks. ... When they cash those in, they'll usually want to buy drugs. ... We're going to be the first people they see."

For a time his mother remained oblivious to his covert activities. "Say I got a thousand dollars' worth of ... jewelry," Biggie claimed. "She'd ask me where the jewelry came from. 'Oh, it's fake. It's not real. ...' She didn't know."

But soon Mrs. Wallace realized that her son was up to no good. He confessed to her that he was dealing crack, and she retaliated by threatening to toss him out of the house. Eventually, they reached an uneasy peace. Biggie would give her money to help out with the bills and household expenses. Voletta would warn him to be careful, but as far as her son was concerned, she couldn't stop his activities.

For a while Biggie even moved out of the neighborhood, hoping to expand his business. Having made some contacts in other parts of the country, he elected to relocate below the Mason-Dixon line. He could make four or five times the money in the Carolinas peddling the same dubious wares he did in Brooklyn, where contraband was easier to obtain. By Biggie's recollection, he spent two years down South. But then he got busted by the local authorities and wound up in jail.

He claims he spent nine months in jail. Finally, he called his mother and confessed that he was in the clink, because she was his only real shot at getting a bondsman and being sprung. Voletta managed to secure a bondsman, and her son was released on $150,000 bail. His disappointed mother ended up squandering the entire settlement from his childhood bus accident on getting her son out of jail.

"When he quit school I wanted to kill him," she said in *Spin*. But now he had a criminal record. Enough was enough. She told him if he wouldn't follow her rules, he couldn't live under her roof. It's a decision she never regretted. People might think she was cold-hearted, but she insisted she'd have done it again in the same circumstances.

Around the same time Biggie started putting his charm and brains to a more productive use. He hooked up with some neighborhood DJs and discovered that he had a substantial talent for rapping over a beat. He started to run with the OGB Crew, the Old Gold Brothers, over on Bedford Avenue. They weren't a rap crew per se, but he hooked up with a DJ dubbed 50 Grand, who had turntables in his basement. 50 Grand would cut up beats and Biggie would get busy on the mike, and they'd tape whatever came out. As people learned about Biggie's rapping talent he began to get more props in the neighborhood.

But he was already considered a player in the 'hood. "Biggie is one of the smartest and funniest guys I know," said *Rap Pages* editor Dream Hampton in a *Spin* story. Hampton grew up living around the corner from him in Bed-Stuy. Even before he'd become a rapper, Wallace's charisma, as well as his formidable stature (he stood six-foot-three and weighed upward of three hundred pounds), made him a center of attention.

Rapper Jay-Z also had grown up in Bed-Stuy; he attended Eli Whitney High while Biggie was at Westinghouse, and the two sometimes crossed paths. Years later, Jay-Z would confess that he was distrustful of most other rappers. "But Biggie was different," he told *The Source*. "He was one of the few people I wanted to hang around and develop a relationship with because he was a funny dude."

Other kids in the neighborhood were drawn by Biggie's charm, yet knew when to step back and stay out of the big man's way. His temper could change from good to ill in a heartbeat, a typical characteristic perhaps, considering his astrological sign—Gemini.

For Biggie, rap was just a hobby, not a way to make money. Mostly, he just got a kick out of hearing his rhymes on tape. Making a record, or getting a deal, didn't enter into the picture. Yet one of his tapes landed in the hands of his neighbor Mister Cee, who was the DJ for Big Daddy Kane (of Cold Chillin' Records renown). Cee thought the tape was so dope that he passed it along to a friend at *The Source* magazine, pushing them to include Biggie in their "Unsigned Hype" column. In turn, the editors of *The Source* were so into him that they asked him to appear on a compilation album of the best "Unsigned Hype" winners. (Although the album never materialized, Common Sense, Mobb Deep, and Back II Back, along with B.I.G., were all slated for inclusion and eventually landed record deals.)

A friend of Puffy's at the magazine passed along a copy of Biggie's demo, and the Uptown A&R VP was smitten. "He had so much melody in his voice," Puffy recalled in *Rolling*

*Stone*. If Mary J. Blige had seasoned her singing with hints of rapping, Biggie laid down his rhymes in a reverse fashion, with such smooth delivery it almost seemed like he was crooning. The way he strung his lyrics together, his writer's eye for detail, and the way he juxtaposed words and ideas also immediately caught Puffy's ear. Remarkably, Biggie didn't even write down his lyrics; he simply made them up off the top of his head and let them incubate in his brain. His descriptions were so vivid, a listener could close his or her eyes and see a whole miniature movie unfurling behind their eyeballs while playing a Biggie track.

The giant man's charisma wasn't lost on Puffy either. He radiated a certain element of mystery, complemented by a magnetic charm that made him the center of attention in any gathering. Clearly, Biggie Smalls was one of a kind, both as a budding artist and as a human being, and all his qualities fused in his unique rhyming style.

But despite his imposing stature, the neophyte rapper from Bed-Stuy was surprisingly low-key. "When I first met Biggie, he was real quiet and shy," Puffy reminisced for *MTV News* on March 28, 1997.

Sometimes he would barely speak at all, and Puffy would have to extract comments from him like a dentist pulling out impacted wisdom teeth. Biggie was just content to observe things around him. Like many people, when success began to overtake him, his life began to seem almost surreal, almost too good to be true. Rather than burst the bubble, he simply sat back and tried to enjoy what happened . . . quietly. In some ways, the caution and hesitation B.I.G. displayed recalled Puffy's demeanor during his earliest days at Uptown. Biggie didn't intend to attract undue attention and get booted out of the party.

Puffy had immediately snapped up Biggie Smalls, rechristened the Notorious B.I.G., to be the first major star on his Bad Boy Entertainment imprint. With the success of Father MC, Jodeci, and Mary J. Blige to Puffy's credit, Biggie knew that his concern needn't be whether or not the records they would make together would dope, but "how dope is it going to be?"

Making the transition to a more respectable lifestyle didn't come easily at first, though. "When I stopped hustling and started making songs, it was the worst," Biggie admitted to *Vibe*. His advance wasn't as substantial as many might have imagined. Peddling crack and firearms had been much more lucrative.

After gradually introducing the Notorious B.I.G. to the public via his Mary J. Blige cameos, a turn on the Heavy D cut "A Buncha Niggas" (on the '92 *Blue Funk* album), the "Party and Bullshit" track (eventually released as a single), and an appearance in Supercat's

"Dolly My Baby" video, Puffy soon set to recording a full-length with him. And like the Uptown artists he'd worked with previously, Biggie soon realized Puffy was a very "hands-on" participant in the recording process.

After the record was in the can, Biggie would talk of how crucial Puffy's role had been, thanks to his experience as seasoned A&R man and producer. Recognizing the musicality of Smalls's delivery, he treated elements of the album as he would a more traditional R&B project, making sure his new star paid attention to how he pitched his voice, or where he breathed in a line. If Puffy didn't think Biggie had done something just right, he'd make the big man lay down the rhyme again . . . and again, until he was completely satisfied.

But before Puffy would have a chance to fully unleash his latest, and greatest, discovery on the public, he'd have a new obstacle to contend with. . . .

## On His Own

Without warning, toward the close of the year, Puffy's boss and mentor, Andre Harrell, dropped a bomb on him; Puffy's employment with Uptown was being terminated, effective immediately. In a word, fired. "It was like the old sensei rejecting the student," Puffy stated matter-of-factly to *Rolling Stone*.

The specific reasons for Combs's dismissal, however, were kept shrouded in mystery. Some sources claimed the two had quarreled over the hiring of a new general manager. Others spread a story that the VP of A&R had acted out of line during a board meeting and been handed the proverbial pink slip by Harrell on the spot.

Eventually, both men would admit that tensions between the two had been increasing for some time. Combs had pressured Harrell to demand more autonomy for Uptown from their parent company, MCA; that was part of his motivation for forming Bad Boy Entertainment in the first place. On the other hand, some insiders suspected that Andre had slowly gotten fed up with how far Puffy had wandered astray from the earlier sound that Uptown had favored, which was more R&B-influenced, soft and traditional.

Puffy would later admit that he had been less than easy to work with on occasions and rubbed people the wrong way. Folks had begun to comment more and more on how he conducted himself—the slow swagger of his gait, his increasingly unflappable confidence. Perhaps he was overstepping his boundaries, even abusing his power.

A few years later, after hard feelings between the two men had subsided, Puffy would look back on his early period at Uptown more favorably. Andre had stood by him through a lot, giving him encouragement and room to grow. "He put his faith in me, and we had a great time," said Puffy in *Rolling Stone* four years after his dismissal.

But a beautiful honeymoon isn't always the precursor to a lasting marriage. Puffy's aspirations had begun to dovetail less smoothly with Uptown's direction. Puffy was so concerned with honing the unique musical sound he'd tapped into, blending harder rhythms with smooth melodic lines and familiar "samples" from older records, that he couldn't fully appreciate the extent to which Uptown's expansion increased the number of concerns Andre had to deal with at a corporate level. As Puffy began acting out, displaying a widening rebellious streak, Harrell had little option but to let him go if Uptown were to continue operating in a harmonious fashion.

Suddenly Puffy was on his own. Like a mother bird pushing her young from the nest to teach them to fly, Andre Harrell knew his protégé was prepared to spread his wings and take solo flight. "All you gotta do to build a star, is know how to make yourself a star," Andre told *Rolling Stone*. Puffy had already proven that he knew how to elevate both himself, and his artists, to impressive heights. When Sean "Puffy" Combs walked into a room, the place lit up.

Harrell felt confident that the twenty-three-year-old Puffy had keen instincts that would bring the world to his feet, regardless of how stubborn he could be, or how much he loved being the center of attention. If need be, Sean Combs knew when to step outside himself and check his ego at the door, if doing so served a greater purpose. Because at the core of his being, Puffy was a winner. And for the first time in his career, he was about to step into the ring alone.

# 7

## Bad Boy Blows Up

The next few months were hellish for Puffy. He would go on crying jags, and even told *Rolling Stone* that he felt like he "wanted to jump off a building" after the firing. He still wasn't completely confident in his abilities and feared that he wasn't ready to step out on his own.

He didn't really have cause to be so distressed, but he couldn't appreciate that just yet. Countless labels were calling to offer him new opportunities, but he couldn't focus on them. It was like trying to reenter the world of dating after a sudden divorce from a long-term marriage; sometimes he felt like he was going crazy.

The most logical step was to take Bad Boy Entertainment and transform it into a much bigger enterprise than it had ever been, or could have become, while still under the Uptown umbrella. Unfortunately, Puffy didn't have the independent resources to pull that off just yet. But what he lacked in funds, he made up for in drive.

In the beginning, Bad Boy didn't even have an office space. Puffy's staff consisted of three young up-and-comers who crashed in his crib. A few years later, in *The Source*, Harve Pierre (who went on to become senior director of black music at RCA Records) recalled that signing on in the early days of Bad Boy was like shipping off to boot camp. Combs insisted that his helpers be out of bed and working by eight A.M. They all shared the same lone computer. And just to make sure they weren't slacking, Puffy required them to fill out a report listing their accomplishments every single day. "I don't think I've ever worked that hard in my life," admitted Pierre.

Puffy's diligence undoubtedly impressed many observers, but his proven talent at developing new artists was the bait that immediately started to lure nibbles from new companies hoping to co-opt Bad Boy and reap some of the benefits of his hit-making abilities. But in the midst of Puffy's lingering depression and uncertainty, the process of finding new financial backers wasn't much fun.

A reprieve came courtesy of his pal L. A. Reid, the noted producer and founder of La-Face Records, as well as the business partner of Babyface (with whom a much younger Puffy had danced in a video). Reid arranged for Puffy to meet with Clive Davis, the president of Arista Records. In addition to working with LaFace, Arista had launched powerhouse performers like Whitney Houston. But that wasn't what really impressed Puffy and made Arista stand out from all the other labels courting Bad Boy.

While most of the people approaching Puffy initiated their negotiations by asking the Bad Boy himself just how much he wanted in cold hard cash for the company, Clive Davis took a different tack. He asked Puffy to tell him about the kind of music he planned on making in the future.

Puffy was very impressed to see that the beats, not the bucks, were Davis's main concern. It was an opinion near and dear to his own heart. Going down in history was much tougher than simply making tons of money, he noted in the May 20, 1995, issue of *Billboard*.

In the press, Clive Davis concurred with Puffy's beliefs that music, and the consistent ability to spot and release quality records, were the key to succeeding in the recording business. In his eyes, Puffy was a distinctive talent with a proven knack for tapping into what people wanted to hear and giving it to them with a fresh flair. "He has a feel for the street and combines it with an unusual grasp of what can best bring it to the marketplace," Davis told *Billboard*. And so, within two months of being dismissed from Uptown, Puffy had signed a $15 million distribution deal for Bad Boy through Arista Records. Always appreciative of the allies around him, he made his mother, Janice, the official owner of Bad Boy Entertainment, to display his gratitude to her for standing by him through thick and thin.

As always, there were skeptics who balked at the deal. "These kids . . . have no idea how to run things," Motown chairman Clarence Avant remarked to *Newsweek* of Puffy and his peers. Detractors claimed that the big companies only nurtured custom labels like Bad Boy or LaFace because it was an inexpensive way for them to get their hands on new talent that the entrenched old-timers were too far out of the loop to catch early on.

Combs didn't worry about what other people thought or said about how he was building his business. He'd already been around the block enough times to know the score. "People are going to say what they will, particularly when you're young, black and successful," he observed in the May 8, 1995, issue of *Newsweek*. He'd already been through the mill more than once as well, but he knew nonetheless that he was in the music industry for the long haul.

Now that Puffy was running the store, he knew he'd have to be a little more accountable for his actions than he had been when Uptown had been behind him. He was already a seasoned entrepreneur and businessman when he made the transition. But up until he had been forced out on his own, he admitted he wasn't in the habit of projecting too far ahead of himself.

Forced to navigate through unfamiliar waters and find a new deal for himself and Bad Boy after leaving Uptown, Puffy had begun to mature quickly. He'd dreamed previously of becoming a modern-day Quincy Jones or Berry Gordy—a black-label executive distinguished by his individual aesthetic, vision, and commitment to a particular sound and a particular business ideal. But while he'd scrutinized the careers of kingpins of that caliber, he hadn't really cobbled together a plan for achieving this goal. Now he'd begun to appraise the full length of the playing field, and was planning accordingly.

In the years that followed, as his successes mounted, he would strive never to lose sight of the idea that the music he loved and championed had the power to bring people together. He'd learned that from Andre Harrell, who'd based Uptown on a similar ideal. "He taught me that my music could be a movement, it could be a lifestyle."

"I didn't come into this business saying, 'I'm gonna look like the biggest black music man,'" he told Veronica Webb. He wanted to be the most important man in pop music, period. Regardless of skin color. He fully intended to make history as a top-notch businessman and music-industry powerhouse. Puffy had limitless praise for his forefathers from the black community who'd made similar dreams come true: Berry Gordy, Andre Harrell. But he wanted to go toe-to-toe with show business's biggest guns: David Geffen, Clive Davis, Steven Spielberg.

Puffy had enjoyed a lot of good fortune, along with his share of bad. But he wasn't going to sit still, not for a minute. And he wouldn't let anyone believe he'd just stumbled into his rising prominence; he made no pretense of being naive. He didn't intend to *attempt* to produce and release hits; he was *going* to produce and release hits, consistently. There was no margin for error. Puffy had dedicated his life to music, and he didn't take the record business lightly, even for one second.

To underscore his determination, he had a motivational plaque hung in the reception area of the new Big Boy Entertainment offices: LIFE IS NOT A GAME.

## The Boy from Brentwood

If there were any doubts in the music arena whether Puffy and Bad Boy Entertainment could stand alone, without the support of Harrell and Uptown, the label's very first release dispelled them. "Flava in Ya Ear" by Craig

Mack went straight into the stratosphere from the Bad Boy launching pad, burning up radio airwaves and crowded dance floors.

Mack originally hailed from Brentwood, Long Island, also the home of Biz Markie, his idol, and EPMD. At the age of seventeen, the young rapper had gained some attention locally as MC EZ, releasing the singles "Get Retarded" and "Just Rhymin' " back in 1987. Unfortunately for Mack, his record label (the legendary Sleeping Bag Records) soon went out of business. It was as if his performing career had never begun. He hung around and graduated high school, but attending college or securing full-time employment wasn't in his stars. And his parents were less than thrilled that their son wanted only to be a rap star.

Luckily, Parrish Smith from EPMD offered Mack work as a roadie on their '92–'93 "Hit Squad" tour, which also featured Redman and Das EFX. Life on the road proved hard ("Das EFX were the only brothers on the tour that was cool with me," Mack told *Vibe*) and his homecoming wasn't much better. Upon his return, his parents kicked him out because he wasn't living up to their expectations. The shock seemed to do the trick, and slowly but surely, Mack began to get his hustle in gear.

At first, Mack was living on the streets or crashing with friends. Then word reached him that an ex-bodyguard for EPMD named Alvin Toney had been hunting around for him.

Toney was launching a new management and production company, and he recalled Mack's verbal dexterity; on the EPMD tour, Toney had discouraged stage-door rappers looking for deals by telling them they had to battle and beat Mack to gain an audience with EPMD. Nobody had ever bested the budding Brentwood b-boy.

Craig hooked up with Toney, who in turn introduced him to Puffy one evening outside of a popular NYC nightclub. Right in front of Mecca, Mack rattled off a freestyle rhyme for Combs. Puffy was impressed and offered to sign Mack, but only if he'd make an appearance on Mary J. Blige's "You Don't Have to Worry." A deal was struck.

Although Mack was originally signed to Uptown, when Puffy was dismissed he was allowed to follow. Puffy had shown faith in the boy from Brentwood, and Mack intended to return the favor. He wasn't discouraged by Bad Boy's brief homeless spell; he felt certain a player of Puffy's magnitude wouldn't be looking for long. Mack's wisdom and trust would pay off.

"Flava in Your Ear" paired Mack's stop-start delivery with a hypnotic groove laid down by Easy Mo Bee, plus lyrical nonstop boasting and even a humorous reference to the cartoon *The Jetsons*. Pumped up by Puffy (who also inserted his own vocal intro), the remix of the track showed off more tongue-twisting tricks from a posse of heavy hitters: Busta Rhymes (to whom Mack was often initially compared), Rampage, LL Cool J, and the Notorious B.I.G.

In the end, the single stayed on the charts for months, eventually attaining platinum sales status. His subsequent album, *Project: Funk da World* would reach number six on the Top R&B Albums chart of *Billboard*, and sell over 500,000 copies. Mack claimed his success could never have happened without Bad Boy and Puffy. "Being with him has been the glass slipper," he declared.

## The New "Bad Girl"

But Craig Mack and B.I.G. weren't the only stars in Puffy's expanding universe. At a session for Al B. Sure!, he'd met a young woman named Faith Evans, a singer, songwriter, and arranger who had worked with Pebbles, Christopher Williams, Usher, and Puffy's previous golden girl, Mary J. Blige. He was instantly impressed by Faith.

Her voice snared his attention right away. It was capable of communicating tremendous emotion without unnecessary theatrics. Even when she was just singing background vocals or doing guide tracks (for other singers to follow), she poured her heart and soul into every note.

But the strength of her character also made an impression on him. A complex woman, Faith would display remarkable resilience when confronted with the slings and arrows critics lobbed at her, claiming she was just a Mary J. Blige knockoff. "I don't mind the comparisons," she said with a shrug to *Vibe*. She knew misinformation was an unfortunate consequence of being a contender. Tales that she was Mary's vocal coach, or took orders from Ms. Blige, were nothing more than rumors. "And I was never anybody's background singer."

Whatever the reason why Puffy found her sound irresistible, Faith soon became the new "bad girl" of Bad Boy Entertainment.

Evans had been born in Lakeside, Florida. When she was just a year old, she moved in with relatives and grew up in a single-family house located in a working-class neighborhood of Newark, New Jersey. Both her mother and her mother's cousin, Johnnie Mae Kennedy, raised her.

Music was a part of Faith's life from a very early age. Her mother, Helene Evans, had sung with a white rock band. The name of the band would fade from Faith's memory, but not the impact of watching her mother perform with them.

Faith herself began singing in church at the age of four. As her name suggests, Faith has deep roots in her religion, and names gospel greats Shirley Murdock and the Clark Sisters as significant stylistic influences. Her "grand-mother" Johnnie Mae Kennedy recounted stories of parishioners leaping to their feet, stamping and hollering, when Faith would sing.

Over the years she expanded her stylistic repertoire, singing with jazz bands and cho-ruses while still attending classes at University High School. Encouraged by her family, she entered—and won—numerous pageants and talent contests. She studied hard and main-tained good grades, and was awarded an aca-demic scholarship to Fordham University in the Bronx.

But after only a year she dropped out. Like Puffy, she didn't want to put off her musical career during four years of college. She did studio work, singing background vocals, and began writing songs. She learned everything she could about the industry.

Along the way she had a liaison of a dif-ferent kind, with its own set of life-altering consequences: Faith was pregnant. She gave birth to her daughter Chyna when she was just nineteen. The father and Faith didn't stick together, but she kept her daughter, and her resolve to provide a good home prompted her to strive even harder to achieve her dreams as an artist. And her diligence paid off; even before she met Puffy, Faith's star was on the rise.

But no matter how promising her fortunes looked from day to day, Faith always aspired to keep a cool head. "I have a lot of friends who are in the business," she would tell the press later. "I've seen people get on their ego tripping and just not even going nowhere." Today's superstar was tomorrow's "where are they now?" profile on the evening news. Faith wasn't egomaniacal by nature, and her roots in the church kept her humble.

In the summer of 1994, after signing with Puffy's label, Faith attended a Bad Boy party. It was there that she met Biggie. She didn't have the slightest idea who the rapper was, or what he was destined for, but she knew their attraction was instantaneous. "He was just such a funny man," she reflected in *Essence*. "He had a real charm about him, a certain style." She was smitten on the spot. When he told her he planned to call, she just smiled. She knew that he didn't have her number, and got the distinct impression that that wasn't about to deter him from phoning her anyway.

When *Vibe* pressed Biggie to explain their attraction, he admitted that of all the women he'd been involved with, Faith had something that set her apart. He couldn't explain it, but that didn't mean he was going to let her slip through his fingers. "I wanted her locked down."

True to his word, Biggie did just that; within two weeks of meeting, the couple was married, on August 4, 1994. Almost immediately tongues began wagging and rumors started to fly about Faith's motives. People suggested that she was just trying to get to his bankroll, which was pretty silly when you paused and thought about the flourishing state of her own career, even before they'd fallen in love. The irony was that even though Biggie's friends and especially his mom were concerned about Faith being a gold digger, his new bride was actually more of a breadwinner than he was.

Biggie laughed at his mother for suggesting something as ludicrous as Faith being after his fortune . . . because he didn't have one yet. And Voletta knew that, because her son owed her money!

No matter. The new, happily married Notorious B.I.G. wouldn't have to worry about his cash flow much longer.

## The Big Man Goes Gold

While Biggie and Faith were honeymooning, Bad Boy dropped the first single from the Notorious B.I.G.'s debut album, entitled *Ready to Die*.

Although Puffy had signed Biggie while he was still with Uptown, his former employers hadn't been interested in keeping the rapper on. Without Puffy, Uptown decided they didn't want to handle B.I.G., so they dropped him. This left B.I.G. unencumbered to make the move to Bad Boy. Anything else would've been unsatisfactory for both men. Puffy had unwavering faith in Biggie's artistry, and the rapper was a hundred percent certain that the big man of Bad Boy was the wisest man to helm his rise to stardom.

Case in point: Biggie had wanted the lead single from his album to be "Machine Gun Funk," but Puffy wouldn't hear of such a notion. He wanted to make some money off this album, and he knew the best plan of action: the first single should be "Juicy." He knew the track, centered around a sample of Mtume's 1983 R&B hit "Juicy Fruit," was bursting with crossover potential, and could probably go gold easily. As a compromise, Puffy let Biggie drop an ill B-side. If "Juicy" was too soft for some players, all they had to do was flip the record and sample the grittier "Unbelievable."

Puffy's killer instincts were right; "Juicy" b/w "Unbelievable" quickly went gold. The Notorious B.I.G.'s debut single rose to number fourteen on the Hot R&B Singles chart, number three on the Hot Rap Singles chart. It even cracked the mainstream Top 40 for ten weeks.

The album followed two months later. Released in October 1994, it was produced primarily by Easy Mo Bee, with additional assistance from the Bluez Bruthas, Jean "Poke"

Oliver of Trakmasters, DJ Premiere, Lord Finesse, and of course, Puffy (also credited as executive producer). Puffy's latest discoveries, the all-girl trio Total, contributed vocals on "One More Chance" and "Juicy," while Method Man matched skills with Biggie on "The What." Diana King, Biggie's old Bed-Stuy posse Junior M.A.F.I.A., and Sean Combs's performing alter ego, Puff Daddy, were on hand, too. The flavor was a mix of R&B grooves, East Coast rhyme skills, and tales of gangsta life.

Given his street pedigree, nobody would accuse B.I.G. of fronting or copping a pose. "Everyday Struggle" recounted a tale from the rapper's illegal dealings across the Mason-Dixon line. Biggie said he was inured to the grim realities illustrated in his tracks; they were everyday occurrences on the streets. He'd seen plenty of men shot in his day. The only time it really stung was when the victim was a friend. Then he would mourn. But just hearing that somebody had gotten blown away barely raised an eyebrow. It came with the territory.

Perhaps if he'd grown up in Mount Vernon, the rapper might have turned out rhymes about mowing the lawn or playing basketball. But Biggie had grown up on Bedford Avenue, watching the brothers sell guns and crack. Art imitates life.

\* \* \*

As always, there were self-appointed moral watchdogs in the media who complained about the grisly content of some of Biggie's lyrics. Yet surprisingly, Puffy would admit years later that he'd made the rapper edit his content from time to time, if the label CEO deemed a rhyme to be in questionable taste. He admitted to Kurt Loder of *MTV News* that he wasn't averse to changing the Notorious B.I.G.'s lyrics if he thought they were unnecessarily harsh for public consumption.

For example, Biggie felt that the robbery scenario of "Gimme the Loot" was just a reflection of the life he'd had to lead in Bed-Stuy. At that point in his life robbing somebody was a viable way to put food on the table in his world. He was just telling a story, spinning a lyrical yarn for the listener's entertainment. But Puffy revealed there had been one line that wouldn't wash with him, where Biggie said, "I don't care that you're pregnant/Gimme the baby rings and the '#1 Mom' pendant." Puffy insisted he modify the lyric. He had to show some consideration for a woman carrying an unborn child.

Yet *Ready to Die* also reflected the complicated nature of the gargantuan rapper's personality and the struggle to reconcile his compassionate side in an era of hard-core gangsta rappers like Tupac Shakur and Snoop Doggy Dogg. "Me & My Bitch" was a realistic (and tragic) love story that reflected Biggie's harsh attitudes toward interpersonal relationships, yet was underscored by sincerity and tenderness: "I swear I hope we fuckin' die together," he rapped.

Listeners connected with the honesty that informed Biggie's rhymes. While other hardcore rappers were too busy relentlessly maintaining their street cred to admit they were vulnerable in any manner, *Spin* observed that Biggie acknowledged the "guilt and shame, as well as the gritty glamour, of 'keeping it real.' " Unlike most of his peers, Biggie appreciated the contradictions of being a hard-core rap icon, a public figure with an unflattering past.

Like much of the album's content, the grim lyrics of the closing "Suicidal Thoughts" were largely autobiographical. Biggie claimed he really meant it when he said he was Ready to Die. Having to wake up every morning and peddle drugs for a living had made him scrutinize his worth as a human being; sometimes he wondered if anyone would genuinely miss him if he was simply wiped off the face of the earth.

Yet at the same time Biggie was wise enough to know there was no real honor in going down like a player. "I'm scared to death," he said to the *Chicago Tribune*. "Scared of getting my brains blown out."

But Biggie would have plenty to live for in the months that followed. Out of the box, *Ready to Die* debuted at number three on the

Top R&B Albums chart, and number fifteen on the *Billboard* 200. It would stay in the charts for many months, eventually attaining gold-record sales status, and generate four hit singles. But these rewards were immaterial to the Notorious B.I.G.

He told Havelock Nelson that every week Puffy told him how many records they'd sold, and then Biggie would shrug and ask if that was especially good. How did his sales stack up against other rappers? He knew that platinum records meant you'd moved more units than gold records did, so he aspired to going platinum. If he could stay on track and keep it real, he'd be able to help out a lot of his old friends—back in Bed-Stuy and beyond—when he blew up big.

Was it hard for Biggie to stay real and still blow up? wondered the writer.

"Naaah." The rapper laughed. "Blowin' up is nothing to me."

## A Son in the Family

As Bad Boy Entertainment blossomed in its first year, Puffy also enjoyed another milestone, albeit one that he doggedly kept out of the spotlight: the birth of his son, Justin. He considered it the highest point of his career to date, because he didn't separate his life, his career, and his music into subdivisions; they were all linked. Young Justin was the finest thing he'd ever produced, the embodiment of everything Bad Boy and bringing people happiness through music meant to Puffy.

The sound of Justin's tiny cries might have been music to Puffy's ears, but the "Wedding March" definitely wasn't on the playlist for the Bad Boy CEO. Justin's mother was Puffy's longtime friend from Mount Vernon, Misa Hylton. The two would remain good friends in the coming years, and Misa obviously had insight into Puffy's inner workings. She told *Rolling Stone* he was the rare sort of individual you could adore and despise simultaneously. Nevertheless, their intimate partnership was short-lived.

Puffy regretted their split, but it was hard to imagine any woman who could compete with his career. The young genius reinforced this notion when *Spin* asked him to describe his ideal woman. "I want a partnership, like Demi Moore and Bruce Willis," he announced. He was seeking somebody who shared a drive as insatiable as his own. Somebody who would support him every step of the way, 24–7, and appreciated a work ethic as strenuous as his. Models might be fun to hang out with, and lovely to look at, but ladies who wanted only to be pretty and sit around the house waiting for Puffy to come home and take them out didn't need to apply for this gig.

He admitted he'd never had a relationship

like the one he dreamed of (although he said he was sorry to have split with Misa). If he had, he said, he'd have tied the knot by now. Waking up every morning, and knowing that a loving family surrounded him, was his greatest dream. Just being a father was a constant source of pride. Watching Justin grow up, and playing a crucial role in shaping his young character, helped Puffy stay sane and centered, rooted on terra firma through the ups and downs of his life.

This was the point he drove home to *Vibe* when they mentioned a rumor, prompted by a scar on his wrist from a mishandled champagne glass, that Puffy had once attempted suicide. He would never kill himself, because he already had too much to live for. "I ain't leaving my son for nobody," he scoffed.

# 8

# Troubles in Paradise

Puffy didn't limit his involvement exclusively to Bad Boy Entertainment projects. As 1994 drew to a close, and the Notorious B.I.G. continued to gain steam, Puffy was also very much in the public eye: he took on an independent production job as the executive producer of Mary J. Blige's hotly anticipated new album, *My Life* (Uptown).

Once again, the two made a killer combination, and Puffy could appreciate why. "No one has sounded as perfect for the music I produce as Mary," he told *Vibe* in 1997. "My tracks were totally made for her, and she was made for my tracks."

But the singer had increased her independence on the new record, too. Other than singing, Mary's contributions to the creative side of *What's the 411?* had been almost nil. She would've liked to play a larger creative role in shaping the material on the first album, but at the time wasn't sure how to go about it. Now she knew the kinds of songs she wanted to sing, the feelings she wished to express.

"Writing is better than being a singer," she said in *Ebony*. And sure enough, Mary made her debut as a vocal arranger and lyricist on the new record, cowriting the vast majority of tracks. She was shedding the insecurity that had held her back in the beginning.

When she had first tried writing songs, she thought the sentiments she was expressing were trite and clichéd, and quickly discarded most of her efforts before they could blossom. "But when I would show the songs to Sean, he was like, 'They're dope,'" she explained to *Essence*. So she kept working at them. And soon she grew to enjoy the discipline of writing her own material.

Mary was also largely responsible for the decision to incorporate samples from artists like Al Green, Rick James, Barry White, Curtis Mayfield, and Roy Ayers into the new recordings. Drawing on those classic tracks reminded her of a special, simpler time. Listening to the records she grew up hearing brought back memories of her family, of her mother and father talking in the quiet of the evening. She wanted to use these musical touchstones to connect the present-day Mary J. to that magical, more innocent era in her life.

That desire permeated her lyrics, too. She examined what people around her were feeling, and what they responded to, and took inspiration from those sources. Most important, she tried to purge some of her own accumulated sadness from the past few years. Stardom had taken her by surprise, and exacted unexpected tolls. By Mary's own account, the tremendous response to *What's the 411?* had completely overwhelmed her, culminating in her "difficult" image.

Andre Harrell concurred with her in *Vibe*, noting that she hadn't been ready, emotionally or mentally, to be scrutinized so extensively and without opportunities to pause and regroup. Under such circumstances, he observed that one of two things typically happened: the artist either lashed out at people or withdrew from the public eye. Blige had done some of both before, but now she was becoming more comfortable with the demands of fame. "More important, she realizes in herself that she truly is the star people think she is."

Mary was doing some damage control: she knew people thought she was a mean person with a sharp tongue, but that wasn't true, and if they gave her a fair shot, they'd see the real Mary shine through. She simply refused to waste her time on people who didn't have her best interests at heart, and she wouldn't deign to answer questions she thought were leading or pointless. In particular, she'd gone to great lengths to keep her romantic relationship with

K-Ci of Jodeci out of the limelight, but it had been a constant struggle.

When she would elaborate on her "bad girl" period, she mentioned over and over how at sea she'd felt during the success of *What's the 411?* and the depression she'd grappled with. But those days were behind her, and she was forging a new, more positive attitude as she continued her climb to the top. And if things were beyond her control, then so be it. She would just put her trust in the Lord, and hope the powers that be would look after her.

Every difficulty life gives us is a lesson, and Mary J. Blige was learning hers. She was going to concentrate on getting what she deserved, and fighting to hold on to it, and push secondary concerns out of her life. "I worked for my success. . . . I deserve this and I'm not giving up," Mary told *Ebony*.

The positive attitude came in handy, as her success continued unabated. Like its predecessor, *My Life* quickly racked up platinum sales status. It also earned a Grammy Award nomination for Best R&B Album. Songs like "All Night Long," "You Gotta Believe," and "You Bring Me Joy" cemented her status as a hip-hop icon. The singles "Be Happy" and a cover of Rose Royce's '77 single "I'm Goin' Down" both hung in the Top 40 for several weeks.

The international popularity of *My Life* allowed her to tour the globe (she was astonished to see legions of Japanese fans dressed like her showing up to the concerts). More important, the money she earned from her hard work allowed her to finally help her family relocate out of the projects.

Mary J. Blige had never dreamed of being a role model or spokesperson for anybody. "Now kids and even grown-ups look up to me because of my music," she recognized in *Essence*. And those were the kinds of rewards that really made her trials and hard-learned lessons worthwhile.

## Gangsta Rap

While Puffy, B.I.G., and Bad Boy Entertainment were blowing up, they weren't the only ones producing the music that became the new sound of young America. Out in California, Marion "Suge" Knight had built his own recording empire: Death Row Records. His stable of artists included heavy hitters like Doctor Dre, Snoop Doggy Dogg, and the hugely popular and influential Tupac Shakur.

The sound of Death Row was considered by many to be the epitome of West Coast hip-hop, both musically and in terms of the lifestyle it reflected and embraced. More than practically any other label, Death Row was synonymous with the genre dubbed "gangsta rap."

In the documentary *Rhyme and Reason*, Los Angeles–based rapper (and ex-con) Ice-T explained how gangsta rap had originally evolved. "While they were having a hip-hop scene in New York, we were having a gang scene." Hence the designation *gangsta rap*. Guns and violence were an intrinsic part of that lifestyle, and the rhymes reflected that reality.

That same honesty extended to other topics as well. A drug dealer would rap from the perspective of a pusher; if somebody was pimping, that's the viewpoint his raps would reveal. The controversial topics of gangsta rap—guns, drugs, "bitches," and "ho's"—were part of gang lifestyle.

Throughout the hip-hop world, raps were a means of staking territory, showing other rappers just how dope you were. But gansta rappers had a much more serious claim: you would listen to what they said, and abide by the law they laid down, or risk the fatal consequences. Morality was a very elastic notion in the world of gangsta rap. "It is reality rap in its truest form," concluded Ice-T, "because you take out all the barricades." It was an exceptionally direct, uncompromising form. And one of the rappers getting the most attention was a man known as 2Pac.

## Tupac on Death Row

Tupac Amaru Shakur (2Pac) wrote songs that delved in unflinching detail into the despair, desperation, and violence of the ghetto. The son of political activists, Tupac had a somewhat unstable home life. He grew up in New York until relocating, as a teenager, first briefly to Baltimore and then to a California ghetto in Marin County, across the bay from San Francisco. Like many young men in his circumstances, he had asserted himself through gangs. By his twentieth birthday, he'd been arrested eight times.

But he was also a volatile and prolific artist. By the time the Notorious B.I.G. released *Ready to Die*, Tupac had made a name for himself with Bay Area posse Digital Underground, released solo albums (*2Pacalypse Now* and *Strictly 4 My N.I.G.G.A.Z.*), and begun to build a reputation as a remarkable actor in films.

Yet he was often in trouble with the law. In March of 1994, he was convicted for assaulting Allen Hughes, director of *Menace II Society*, in a 1992 fistfight. In 1993, he was arrested in Atlanta in connection with the shooting of two off-duty police officers. Vice President Al Gore even got into the act, claiming that Shakur's inflammatory lyrics on *2Pacalypse Now*—cuts like "Brenda's Got a Baby"—had played an influential role in the killing of a Texas policeman.

Tupac recorded exclusively for Death Row, run by controversial figure Marion "Suge" Knight. Before entering the music business,

Knight had been a football player (he'd played briefly for the L.A. Rams). While employed as a bodyguard for R&B singer Bobby Brown, he'd gotten a behind-the-scenes look at the West Coast rap world and begun to appreciate the financial rewards to be reaped there. But from the beginning, his Death Row label had been distinguished by the air of violence that surrounded it. Knight had purportedly secured his first three artists—Doctor Dre, The D.O.C., and Michel'le—after intimidating Eazy-E of Ruthless Records (who previously held their contracts) with threats of baseball bats and pipes.

Suge would boast that the label was named Death Row because almost everybody involved with it had tangled with the law. Later on, federal investigators would begin to look into how Knight had raised the cash to start up a label in the first place; many suspected the capital could be directly linked to the drug trade or organized crime. Regardless, Knight had signed the artists required to put Death Row on the map, and by 1995 they were the largest rap label in the world. For the time being . . .

For his part, Puffy wasn't interested in being too closely associated with gangsta rap. He could appreciate the legitimacy of what its artists were trying to communicate—especially in light of the history of the Notorious B.I.G.—

but he didn't want to encourage reckless gang-banging on wax just to turn a profit.

Puffy realized that the best rappers drew on their own personal experiences and on their observations of their environment. "I think there's room for people from the street to be able to voice their opinion," he told *Just for Black Men*.

He added that Bad Boy artists didn't try to glorify gangsta culture, or anything too hard-core, in their lyrics. Puffy appreciated how gruesome reality was, especially in the poorest neighborhoods of the inner city, but he thought that people needed to hear something besides a repetition of the ugly truth. He wanted to nurture artists who would entertain people's dreams, no matter what environment they sprang from.

As far as Puffy was concerned, even if he wanted to be the brightest and the best, there was plenty of room for everyone to play in the sandbox. And he looked up to Marion "Suge" Knight a tremendous amount. Death Row had already been firmly established when Bad Boy finally took shape, and Puffy learned from its example.

Death Row represented the type of company Puffy wanted to helm, even if he disliked the politics of his West Coast rivals. He wanted Bad Boy to emulate other labels founded and run by black men that had provided the soundtrack for a lifestyle movement, like Def Jam, Motown, or Philadelphia International. Bad Boy would be the sound of a specific culture.

And so the relationship between all the major players at both labels was initially quite cordial. If Knight visited New York, he'd swing by the Bad Boy offices and drop in on Puffy. And if business took Puffy to Los Angeles, he would run with Suge and his gang. He'd even kicked back at Snoop Doggy Dogg's crib on a couple of occasions. Never in a million years did he imagine the friendly competition between the two companies might devolve into something much uglier.

Meanwhile, Biggie had become close to Tupac. The two men had met in 1993, when the West Coast rapper was appearing in John Singleton's 1993 movie *Poetic Justice*, starring Janet Jackson. Tupac kept playing Biggie's "Party and Bullshit" single on the set. Later they met at Tupac's L.A. home, where they hung out and chilled. Biggie told *Vibe* they'd clicked so quickly, and stayed cool since, because both men were Geminis who understood the mercurial nature of each other's ever-changing personalities.

"Biggie loved him to death," Puffy confessed in *Vibe*. And in the early days of Bad Boy, at the start of Biggie's career, Tupac had even given the company a chance to improve its visibility. The Notorious B.I.G. had been

Tupac's opening act on numerous bills. Combs stressed in print how grateful he and Biggie had been for Tupac's support early on.

But the relationship between the four men and their labels would begin to erode following an incident in November of 1994, escalating into one of the bitterest rivalries of recent years.

## The Attack on Tupac

In the middle of November the year before, a nineteen-year old Manhattan woman named Ayanna Jackson claimed that Tupac and two of his associates had sexually assaulted her in a hotel room. Jackson pressed charges against the three men, and the rapper had stood trial.

On November 30, 1994, Tupac was back in Manhattan to face sentencing. Shortly after midnight on the jury's first day of deliberation, he and some of his crew headed to the Quad Studios in Times Square. The West Coast rapper had agreed to work on a track with East Coast rapper Little Shawn (who for a time was affiliated with Uptown Entertainment).

Upon entering the lobby of the building, the entourage was ambushed. They had noticed two men dressed in army fatigues (which Tupac identified as gang garb favored in Brooklyn) loitering around the entrance; a third assailant was waiting in the lobby, pretending to read a newspaper. As the group approached the elevator bank the two men in fatigues, armed with identical handguns, bore down on them, ordering Tupac to the floor and demanding that he surrender his jewelry and money. The man who'd been hiding behind the paper held a pistol on one of Tupac's four companions, rapper Randy "Stretch" Walker.

When Tupac went for his own gun (hidden in his waistband), they began firing. Then they began to beat him, tearing the jewelry from his body. Then they started shooting again. He was hit a total of five times: in his left arm, chest, head, thigh, and groin. His attackers made off with $40,000 worth of jewelry.

His party dragged Tupac, bleeding from his wounds, upstairs, to a studio where they knew Biggie was supposed to be recording. There, they found B.I.G., Puffy, and Andre Harrell.

Puffy claimed that he immediately raced to Tupac's side, tried to calm him down and keep him still, all the while barking for somebody to call an ambulance. Paramedics arrived and took him to a nearby hospital. His prognosis was good; he would live. Biggie came to visit him the next afternoon. After surgery that same day Tupac checked himself out of the hospital, fearful that his attacker might seek him out to finish the job. He recovered at the New York home of his actress friend Jasmine Guy.

Puffy, the Notorious B.I.G., and Lil' Kim (from Junior M.A.F.I.A.) collecting prizes for *Ready to Die* at the 1995 Billboard Music Awards.

Who's got who in check? Puffy and Busta Rhymes catch the Wyclef Jean show at Tramps in Manhattan.

Cool by the pool: Puffy and the men of Jodeci relaxing in the spring of 1993.

Puffy takes time out from his hectic schedule to check out the premiere of *Scream 2* in the summer of 1997.

Uptown in Harlem with Puffy, young Justin Combs, and Faith Evans on the set of the "We'll Always Love Big Poppa" video shoot, April 1997.

Puff Daddy and special guest star Sting perform their tribute to the late Notorious B.I.G. at the 1997 MTV Music Video Awards.

Puff Daddy pours his heart out performing "I'll Be Missing You" at the MTV Music Video Awards, September 4, 1997.

Puff Daddy and Faith Evans at the podium at the 1997 MTV Music Video Awards.

Puffy and Biggie's mom, Voletta Wallace, accept the late rapper's prize for "Hypnotize" at the 1997 MTV Music Video Awards.

© Frank Micelotta/Outline

Puff Daddy hanging at the MTV Movie Awards in June 1997.

© Barry King/Gamma Liaison

Puffy's budding superstar Mase, on the set of Lox's "We'll Always Love Big Poppa" video shoot.

Puffy sends
wishes of peace
to his fans
around the world.

When millionaires
meet: Puffy and
Donald Trump at
the opening of
Justin's, July 1997.

## Troubles in Paradise

On December 1, Tupac was sentenced to serve two and a half years at the Clinton Correctional Facility in Dannemora, New York. In light of the fact that the twenty-two-year-old rapper hadn't been convicted of rape, but rather a lesser sexual violation, many were astonished that he was being sent to a maximum-security prison.

Shortly after his imprisonment, Tupac announced in an interview with *Vibe* that he suspected Puffy and Biggie had arranged his shooting. He claimed that when he'd been ushered into the studio that night, he'd seen about forty people there. Contrary to Puffy's testimony, Shakur said nobody came forward to help him. "I noticed that nobody would look at me," he told *Vibe*. He insinuated that all assembled knew that he was going to be shot.

Puffy was flabbergasted by these accusations. It was unthinkable to him that he would assist in such an assault on anybody, friend or foe. Besides, he'd been in this line of work long enough to realize that if he were to set somebody up like that, staying in town wouldn't be advisable. Maybe if he'd been in South America at the time of the attack, it would have rung truer. But he was waiting in the same building as Tupac. The charges seemed bitter and hollow.

When Tupac's accusations ran in the April 1995 issue of *Vibe*, Puffy tried to maintain a level head, although he was astonished by the claims. His reason for being at Quad that night was the same as Biggie and Tupac's; he was participating in a recording session. "[We] had no knowledge of him going to be robbed," he later reiterated to Kurt Loder of *MTV News*. Anything else was just a fantasy born from an overactive imagination, nothing short of a bold-faced lie.

Biggie in particular was stunned by Tupac's claims. The rap kingpins from opposite coasts had shared some good times. Biggie considered Tupac his friend, and wouldn't have lifted a finger to hurt him.

Puffy wrote to Shakur in prison, hoping to clear the air of any suspicions or hard feelings. He asked if he could come visit, and get to the bottom of what had been published in *Vibe*. Biggie and Puffy wanted Tupac to know they had nothing but love in their hearts for him.

And Shakur supposedly responded, telling Puffy not to worry, that they were cool. He didn't want the boys to come visit him in the big house, but they didn't need to worry about bad blood. Puffy and Biggie heaved a sigh of relief, taking Tupac's response to mean he didn't want the matter blown out of proportion. They went about their business, and hoped Tupac would be released from jail soon, and all parties involved could resume business as usual.

They thought there was nothing to worry

about between Bad Boy and Death Row. But they were wrong. Dead wrong.

## The Total Image

In April, Puffy unveiled "Can't You See," the first single from the all-female vocal trio Total. The track was lifted from the soundtrack to the movie *New Jersey Drive* (a drama about carjacking in Newark, executive-produced by Spike Lee). Featuring an able assist from the Notorious B.I.G., whom Total had already backed on "Juicy" and "One More Chance," the track (which incorporated a sample from James Brown's "The Payback") stayed on the *Billboard* charts for fourteen solid weeks, peaking at number thirteen.

The women of Total were named Kima, Pam, and Keisha. Pam and Kima had both grown up in New Jersey and knew each other since the ninth grade. Pam loved to sing, and leaped at the chance to do so whenever she could. Eventually, she persuaded Kima—who had planned on studying cosmetology—to join her in a career in music. A few years later they roped in Keisha (who also hailed from New Jersey), and Total was born.

In 1992, the threesome was working hard, trying to gain recognition and singing at gigs in the Bronx, when they came to the attention of Sybil Pennix. Pennix was a manager and stylist who'd been instrumental in developing Mary J. Blige's savvy but streetwise image (she also made a vocal cameo on B.I.G.'s "Me & My Bitch"). She took Total under her wing, and soon brought them to someone she felt sure would appreciate their good looks and talent: Puffy.

Their audition for Puffy happened on such short notice that the girls didn't even have a chance to rehearse, so they went through their paces as they rode in the elevator of the Hit Factory. They knew they'd done okay later that same day, though, when Puffy rang up Pennix and told her not to let anyone else sign the girls until he could make the most of this opportunity. When Bad Boy split from Uptown, Total came along.

Puffy and Pennix introduced the group slowly, first with a spot in Erick Sermon's "Hit and Switches" video, and then with spots on the *Ready to Die* singles. "Can't You See" was written and produced by Puffy. They would be Bad Boy's answer to successful girl groups like TLC (whom Puffy had worked with in the past) and En Vogue.

"Total is really made up of three lead singers, and each one can hold her own," Puffy announced in a press release. "But they have an incredible rapport with each other in the studio which comes across in their music."

For their part, the three seemed grateful for the tutelage and image shaping. Kima explained in *Vibe* that she felt like she'd had two upbringings. "By my mother, who raised me to have morals, and then again by Puffy and Sybil, who taught us to deal with the craziness of this business." They seemed prepared to avoid some of the pitfalls that Mary J. Blige had faced, and appreciated the importance of being assisted by seasoned hands.

Sure enough, critics would compare their sound with many of Puffy's earlier acts, including Mary J. Blige and Jodeci. The women of Total were nonchalant about this. They didn't care what people said they sounded like as long as they got the public's attention. And as always, presentation was an essential part of the package. "When you hear our music you can't help but feel the attitude within us," Pam declared.

About the same time Total was breaking out, Puffy and Biggie traveled to California for the 1995 Soul Train Music Awards, held in Los Angeles. Puffy would recall the evening fondly in later months to *Spin*. The program was being filmed live for television. The duo was just about to perform. A lot of money had been sunk into the production budget, the whole crew was waiting. . . .

And Biggie didn't like the shoes he was wearing.

Puffy got down on his knees and begged his friend not to worry about his footwear now, just to get on the performance. But now the rapper was buggin' on his shoes. His were always tight, he complained. Why couldn't he find the right ones to fit his oversize feet?

Finally, Biggie convinced one of their heavy-set bodyguards to swap with him. During the performance, Puffy admitted he had trouble containing his laughter. He couldn't believe how outrageous Biggie could be. "Like, this is my man, and he crazy!"

But as with all his artists, from Mary J. Blige to Total, Puffy had cultivated Biggie's taste for the finer things in life and integrated them into his image: designer clothes, big cars, and multiple magnums of Cristal champagne. In *Interview*, supermodel Veronica Webb applauded Puffy for creating a whole new brand of style that simultaneously embraced and rejected elements of high-fashion chic.

"No other nigger out there can say they're ghetto-fabulous," exclaimed Puffy. "I'm ghetto-fabulous." He claimed he could cruise down Fifth Avenue in a Rolls-Royce, hip-hop booming out of the sound system, then strut into Gucci and buy the whole store in one fell swoop. And for an encore, if he cared to, he might swing through Harlem, do a twirl on 125th Street, and pass out Benjamins to homeless people on the way back.

And yet, coming from the streets, weren't the artists sending mixed messages to the fans by emphasizing material gain as a primary measure of success? Biggie told *Spin* he didn't think so. He believed his boasts about owning the most fly gear in the 'hood inspired other brothers to go out and work to make money so they could afford the latest fashions. He motivated people to reach for the stars . . . or at least a nicer pair of sneakers. Was that so wrong?

### The Magic Touch

Throughout the summer, Bad Boy kept delivering the hits. On the heels of Total, Biggie dropped his third hit single from *Ready to Die*. In January, "Big Poppa" had peaked at number six on the charts; now "One More Chance/Stay with Me" (which interpolated the DeBarge tune "Stay with Me" into the track), with "The What" featuring Redman on the flip, began an extended stay at the top of the chart. For nine weeks it was the number-one R&B single, according to *Billboard*.

"It's the distinctive sound of his voice and melodies that sticks in your head," explained Puffy when quizzed about the secret of B.I.G.'s success, in the July 1, 1995, issue of *Billboard*. "He's making good records, and he's getting better and better with time." Like all the best Bad Boy acts, he held appeal for hip-hop *and* R&B fans. "He has a straight-up black sound," said Puffy, "like somebody's big black uncle from Brooklyn."

Just a few weeks later Faith (who sang backing vocals on the B.I.G. song) made her own chart debut. "You Used to Love Me," released in July, got to the number twenty-four spot.

With so many consecutive successes under his belt, plus his high public profile via countless cameos on wax and in his artists' videos, the industry and the media were taking greater notice of Sean "Puffy" Combs. During 1995, magazines from *Billboard* to *Paper* and *Rolling Stone* to *Newsweek* would run features on his growing prominence in the music world.

Craig Mack and the Notorious B.I.G. had both dropped when there was nothing like them in the marketplace. Puffy wasn't afraid to take chances, as long as he'd done his homework and was wholly confident that his records would connect with hungry listeners. To ensure their success, he'd also concentrated on unique marketing methods, from picketing in front of radio stations to advertising via the Goodyear blimp. Every aspect of Bad Boy focused on Puffy's creed to give people quality entertainment.

*Billboard* illustrated the extent of his success by noting that in one week of the spring, four of Puffy's productions had been in the Top 20 of the Hot R&B Singles chart: the Notorious B.I.G.'s "Big Poppa," Usher's "Think of You," Mary J. Blige's "I'm Goin' Down," and Total's premiere jam "Can't You See."

For such a young company, with a fairly green team of employees, Bad Boy's returns were especially impressive. Even Puffy was amazed at how well things were going. He had thought that it might take a while to build up a full head of steam, but enthusiasm was giving the company an extra shot in the arm, and he felt confident the music's appeal would level out any unexpected dropping of the ball by unseasoned staffers.

Just as Puffy never intended to make a mediocre record, he couldn't foresee Bad Boy ever heading in any direction but up, up, up. But he wasn't afraid of learning from mistakes, either. "That keeps a really aggressive atmosphere here and empowers people to do their jobs," he noted in the May 20, 1995, *Billboard*.

Puffy also maintained certain traditions he himself had benefited from not so long before. The Bad Boy team included plenty of interns—not just high-school and college students, but even kids off the streets hoping to break into the music business. Puffy got angry when people called him a "boy wonder." He was unique, but there were other young entrepreneurs like him, who could equal his feats if given similar opportunities. "The one single thing that makes me mad is when people describe me as 'a boy wonder,' " he stressed. "[The kids] just need the chance, and that's what I'm trying to give them at Bad Boy," he told *Billboard*.

Almost all the articles profiling Puffy emphasized his meticulous attention to detail at Bad Boy, his gift for micromanagement, whether in the office or while working on a project. "As he talks, he barks orders to the young men and women who walk through the studio," noted *Newsweek*. Puffy knew what type of stationery his assistant needed, where the new chairs were going in the lobby, what outfit Faith Evans should wear to her photo shoot.

And every time he instructed somebody to do something, he'd politely add, "Thank you."

Puffy knew that not everyone was thrilled by his triumph. There were plenty of people who thought he was too cocky, who couldn't wait to see him stumble and fall hard. He wasn't discouraged by the prospect. He didn't get preoccupied with the opinions of others. He had too much work to do.

As a producer, he was lending "the magic Puffy touch" to everyone from TLC to Shabba Ranks. Biggie was cleaning up on the road, and Faith and Total were recording their debut albums. Bad Boy's new male vocal quartet—112—was taking shape, and there was talk of Puffy's involvement in LL Cool J's latest comeback.

His goals didn't end there. In *Rolling Stone*, he hinted that he planned on releasing his own full-length recording bow soon. He bragged that he was going to call it *Puff Daddy's Greatest Hits* even though it was a brand-new release. He liked to do things that way. "Just some arrogant shit straight out of the box."

**9**

# From Bad to Worse

While Puffy and Bad Boy kept blowing up bigger and bigger throughout 1995, Biggie unveiled his own bad creation that same summer. Junior M.A.F.I.A. (short for "Masters At Finding Intelligent Attitudes") was a posse of Biggie's old Bed-Stuy homies. They dropped in July with a single called "Player's Anthem," featuring a sample of the old Kurtis Blow jam "Lodi Dodi." Rounded out with a rap from B.I.G., the track quickly raced up the charts, becoming the "summer's biggest street-buzz hip-hop record," according to *Entertainment Weekly*. A few weeks later their debut full-length, *Conspiracy*, followed. Both quickly sold gold.

Although Biggie rapped on four out of fifteen cuts, he was careful not to overshadow the M.A.F.I.A.'s formidable stable of talent. The collective comprised four separate acts: the Sixes (Little Caesar, Chico, and Nino Brown), the Snakes (Trife and Larceny), and solo MC's Klepto and Little Kim.

"[Junior M.A.F.I.A.] is simply everyone in the crew hitting you from a different angle, trying to get their point across," explained Trife. Where the Sixes were playful, the Snakes were deadly serious, representing the hard-edged callousness of an increasing number of disenfranchised American youths. MC Klepto lived up to his name with tongue-twisting tales of hustling and getting into trouble.

All of them had known Biggie since his days as a neighborhood dealer. He had encouraged the various M.A.F.I.A. members, and swore that when he broke out he'd come back for them. He saw too much of himself in them not to. When Biggie looked at his protégé and sidekick Little Caesar, and how his life was screwed up, hanging by a thread, it harkened back to his own not-so-distant days in Bed-Stuy. "Kids can be so mean," Biggie observed in *Vibe*. "They'll tease the shit out of you if your shit is anything less than what they got."

Caesar hadn't been in school, hadn't been doing much of anything . . . till Biggie brought him under his wing and encouraged him. "Now he got a $700 leather coat, diamond rings, and a record deal," noted the big-hearted rapper.

Lil' Kim said in *Details* that she'd lived on the same Bed-Stuy block as Biggie, and that they'd taken to rhyming together, just for kicks. By 1992, he'd convinced Kim she should concentrate on honing her rapping skills. When *Ready to Die* took off, she was still struggling; none of the M.A.F.I.A. had progressed much. So Biggie came back to claim the cohorts he'd left behind. "And I was happy he kept his word," Lil' Kim told *Details*, "because only friends keep their promises."

"We admire B.I.G. for taking us up from the street with him," said Klepto. They knew he didn't have to do so. "You gotta give him props for that."

But Biggie said the chance to help his friends had motivated him to keep rapping. "We was all doin' illegal shit, but one person out of the crew got in here, so that's my job now, to drag everybody in."

"They my peeps," he added in *Vibe*. "They rollin' with me." No wonder they called him Big Poppa.

Playing Big Momma to Smalls's Poppa Bear was Lil' Kim, whose emerging talent on the mic ignited "Player's Anthem," "Get Money," and "Backstabbers." She'd only been a shy seventeen-year-old when he met her and talked her into trying her luck as a rapper. But by the time *Conspiracy* had gone gold, he'd convinced the only female member of the nine-strong crew that she should launch a solo career.

She'd been born Kim Jones, in Bed-Stuy.

Her father, Linwood, was a bus driver and former army sergeant. Her mother, Ruby Mae, was a housewife who'd left the family when Kim was nine. Her daughter understood; her father was a demanding man to live with, and if she could have, she would have followed Ruby Mae.

Kim and her brother Christopher remained with their dad, but sometimes his strict discipline was more than they could handle. In the mornings, he'd wake Kim by banging a big stick against the headboard of her bed. Finally, the tense situation between them came to an ugly head. She confessed in *Details* that her father had tossed her out of their home at age fifteen. Finding food or a place to sleep became a struggle for her. She knew all too well what it was like to be hungry and tired, with only twenty-five cents in your pocket.

During the hard times, she stayed with friends, and made what little money she could as a drug courier. But even then, she had certain boundaries. She later told *People* that she never actually sold on the street. "I used to help the guys cut it up," she admitted, but she'd only done it to survive. "I'm surprised it didn't wreck my life."

This was how she initially met Biggie. The more they ran into each other on the streets, they closer they became. But just how close they became would be a source of joy and irritation for different parties in the years and months to come.

### The East Coast/West Coast Rivalry

In August, it became apparent to Puffy that Tupac's accusations in *Vibe* concerning his shooting the previous autumn were not an isolated incident. The state of affairs between Bad Boy Entertainment, Death Row Records, and their respective star artists was becoming something much nastier than "friendly competition."

The turning point came during *The Source* magazine awards, held at the Paramount Theater in Manhattan. From the stage, for all assembled to hear, Suge Knight remarked, "If you don't want the owner of your label on your album or in your video or on your tour, come sign with Death Row." The comment was clearly directed at Puffy, who had maintained his high profile with cameos in most of the Bad Boy videos.

Combs was astonished. He couldn't believe a man he counted as a close friend would belittle him publicly like this. Still, when it came time for him to present an award, he took a moment to talk about unity between the scenes on the East and West coasts. When the winner was announced, he made a point of hugging the recipient: Death Row star Snoop Doggy Dogg.

But Knight's inflammatory words soon spread through the hip-hop community, sowing seeds of dissent. Then the situation intensified a month later, on September 24, 1995, when members of the Bad Boy family, including Biggie, Puffy, and the Junior M.A.F.I.A., headed to Atlanta for a birthday celebration in honor of fellow superstar R&B producer Jermaine Dupri.

In an extended interview, given months later, Puffy swore to *Vibe* that he wasn't concerned about encountering any hostilities; he'd even brought his young son, Justin, to Atlanta with him. And despite rumors to the contrary, he wasn't protected by bodyguards. After hanging out at the postparty, hosted at a club called Platinum House, Puffy decided to split. He was waiting out front for his limousine to come around, chatting up some ladies.

He insisted that he hadn't seen Suge go into the club. Later he heard that Suge got into a disagreement with some of the other patrons. Puffy knew most of the people in the club, but he didn't know who Suge was mad at, or what the argument concerned—none of the details, save that Suge had crossed swords with someone in the bar.

Next thing he knew, guests began pouring out of the club. Puffy heard people yelling and screaming, and saw people he knew—including Suge—exiting. Puffy claims he got back out of his car, and went up to Suge, asking if he was all right. He maintained he was only offering assistance to a friend.

Puffy was facing Suge, trying to ascertain what was going down. Suddenly they heard shots ring out. Puffy whipped around, and they both saw a man go down to the ground. Puffy reminded *Vibe* that his back had been turned in the direction the shots came from. "I could've got shot, and [Suge] could've got shot."

But the man on the ground was Jake Robles, a Death Row employee and one of Knight's closest friends. Puffy said the Death Row CEO accused him of foul play right there on the spot: "I think you had something to do with this."

Puffy couldn't believe what he was hearing. He'd been standing right in front of Suge when the shooting happened.

Robles died in the hospital a week later. Some witnesses claimed in the press that a member of the Bad Boy entourage was responsible. And Suge believed them.

To this day, Puffy balks at such a crass suggestion. He told *Rolling Stone* such an accusation was lunacy. He had far too much invested in this life to risk losing it all by tampering with human lives. Besides, his faith in God was far too strong to lead him that far astray. Puffy didn't want to meet his Maker with blood on his hands.

## From Bad to Worse

* * *

After serving eleven months hard time at the Clinton Correctional Institute, Tupac Shakur was finally released. He'd been sprung through the doings of Suge Knight. While in prison, Shakur (who'd been signed to Interscope Records previously) told Knight how desperate he was to regain his freedom, but that he also planned on turning over a new leaf and severing his ties to thug life, if he got out.

Knight and Shakur struck a deal; the rapper signed a four-page, handwritten recording contract, guaranteeing his next three records to Death Row and making Death Row's longtime attorney David Kenner his own counsel. In exchange, Knight posted the $1.4 million bond required to secure Tupac's release while his appeal for the conviction was pending.

The night he emerged from his incarceration, Tupac flew back to Los Angeles on a plane chartered by Suge Knight. That very evening, he entered an L.A. studio and began work on his first Death Row album. Within three days he'd recorded seven songs.

Meanwhile, tensions between the Death Row camp and Bad Boy Entertainment continued to escalate. Hip-hop playas and fans on both coasts began to wonder if a state of war loomed on the horizon. *The New York Times* reported that after the murder of Jake Robles, Puffy dispatched Mustafa Farrakhan, the son of powerful black leader Louis Farrakhan, to attempt to defuse the situation with Knight. Puffy later told *Vibe* he didn't actually ask Farrakhan to go, but did tell him that if he could do anything to bring about an end to the feud, he had Puffy's blessing. The Death Row CEO reportedly refused to meet with the emissary.

A few weeks later, at a rap conference in Miami, rumors circulated that both Suge (who had never concealed earlier affiliations with the Bloods, an infamous L.A. gang) and Puffy were bringing armies from the underworld to exact revenge. When Puffy failed to attend the conference, *Billboard* wrote that he'd been intimidated by threats from Death Row.

In December, while filming a video for their track "New York, New York" in Red Hook, Brooklyn, shots were fired at the trailer of Death Row artists Tha Dogg Pound. The clip had featured enormous West Coast rappers flattening the Big Apple à la Godzilla. A posse of New York MCs then released a response record, "L.A., L.A.," with stand-ins for members of Tha Dogg Pound being abducted, tortured, and eventually thrown off a bridge.

## Everyday Struggle

It was no secret in music-industry circles that for all their passion, the union of Faith Evans and Biggie Smalls was definitely showing strains at the seams. There was much they hadn't learned about each other during their whirlwind courtship, and the married life of two rising stars was filled with obstacles.

Almost immediately after tying the knot, Biggie had hit the road touring. Meanwhile, Faith remained in New York, recording her album. Being apart from her husband was almost more than she could stand.

After that round of commitments, B.I.G. had gotten embroiled in making the Junior M.A.F.I.A. record. As their first anniversary came and passed Faith complained that Biggie seemed to be getting caught up in his larger-than-life image. "But I couldn't see myself being without him," she confessed to *Vibe*.

She loved to cook, and Biggie liked few things better than to enjoy her fare. They both spoke of opening a restaurant together when their twilight years approached and performing was no longer an option. But Faith had a will as strong as her husband's. After one argument, she augmented one of her tattoos, so that instead of reading "Big," it would read "Big Faye." "That definitely made a statement," she told *Essence*.

On another occasion, when Biggie was performing in Virginia while Faith was in New York, they got into an argument over the phone. Biggie hung up and refused to answer when his wife tried calling back. Later, after his set, a gaggle of groupies came back to his room and paired off with some of his boys. There was one odd girl out, and Biggie permitted her to sleep in his room. Nothing more; Biggie insisted it was all completely innocent.

The next morning, a knock on the door awakened them. Thinking it was housekeeping, the female guest opened the door, and Faith pounced on her. "Punched homegirl in the face about 30 times, then got on the next flight back to New York," Biggie recalled, having watched the entire affair from the bed. He took the hint and headed straight back to New York to patch things up.

The two ran hot and cold, often in the same discussion. They were almost like little children in the way they could battle, then make up, in a matter of minutes. They would have fights that would've destroyed any other couple—yet theirs seemed to fortify their commitment to one another.

Meanwhile there was talk that Biggie and Lil' Kim were knockin' boots. As a member of Junior M.A.F.I.A., she was often on the road with the rapper. And in *Details*, Kim would later tell readers that she'd known Biggie long before Faith. "It's hard to let go of something you had." She said Biggie had asked her to marry him before proposing to Faith, and that she had declined.

As for the claim that they were having an affair while Biggie and Faith were a couple, Kim would never deal with it explicitly. She refused to divulge too many details. "I know what the relationship that me and Biggie had was and I was there way before anyone else and that's that!" she barked at writer Brantly Bardin of *Details*.

In October of 1995, Faith Evans was in Los Angeles, writing songs for Tha Truth, an R&B group. During her stay, she met Tupac Shakur. "He was mad cool," Faith admitted in *Vibe*. They ran into each other at a party or two and shared drinks with a few of Faith's friends. She recalled how fondly Biggie had spoken of Tupac, and treated him cordially. The rapper extended an invitation to her to sing on his forthcoming album. She agreed (pending approval from Bad Boy) and, before returning to New York, recorded a rough vocal track for him.

The next thing she knew, rumors were flying that she and Tupac were having an affair. People said she was even carrying his child. Suge Knight claimed in a *New York Times* magazine article that Faith had bought Tupac an expensive suit on a wild shopping spree; some suggested she'd even hocked her wedding ring to pay for it.

(Meanwhile an equally vicious story that Suge and Puffy's ex-girlfriend Misa Hylton were an item began to make the rounds. Death Row purportedly went so far as to draw up an advertisement featuring a picture of Misa and Suge holding Puffy's two-year-old son, Justin.

The caption supposedly read, "The East Coast can't even take care of their own." But despite the talk, no ad materialized, and Death Row quickly denied it had ever existed.)

Faith conceded that she had heard the rumors and maintained that she and Tupac had never slept together. She never even saw him again after she left Los Angeles. Meanwhile, Tupac continued to fan the flames by making remarks like "you know I don't kiss and tell" in *The Source*.

Though he remained silent on the matter for a long time, when Biggie finally did address the topic, he chastised Tupac for tarnishing Faith's reputation, even though he and Faith were estranged by that time. Prior to the rumors, there had been no grounds for animosity between Tupac and Faith, and Biggie argued that if they had slept together, Tupac was being even more disrespectful to her. It didn't add up for Tupac to seduce Faith to get back at Biggie, then hurt her, not him. It didn't make sense for him to damage Faith's reputation, especially if she and her husband were on the outs. "That's why I don't believe it," Biggie told *Vibe*, referring to the alleged affair.

The following January, Death Row contacted Bad Boy via the mail and requested clearance for Faith to sing on the record. No agreement was reached. Soon she began to hear from friends that her vocal had turned up on the track "Wonda Why They Call U Bytch?"

on Tupac's new album *All Eyez on Me*. Death Row claimed the singer was a vocalist named Jewell.

## Facing Off on the West Coast

In March of 1996, the Bad Boy family headed west for the Soul Train Music Awards. Rivalry or no, they weren't going to be scared out of Los Angeles. But when Biggie won and got up to accept his award, and gave a shout out to Brooklyn, the assembled crowd hissed.

After the show, Tupac and Biggie ran into each other in person, squaring off in the parking lot. It was their first encounter since the day after Shakur's shooting in November of 1994.

A week later, the *Hollywood Reporter* published an anonymous source who said Shakur had threatened Biggie with a pistol; Biggie said that wasn't the case, although Tupac and his boys, who were accompanied by Knight, had presented an intimidating threat regardless. Biggie admitted in *Vibe* that he was duly impressed by the deadly serious fashion in which they'd conducted themselves. "They made everything seem so dramatic."

The moment of tension broke when Little Caesar, drunk, started flying off, rallying for the East Coast. Tupac pointed out that they were on hostile, West Coast territory. A showdown seemed inevitable. In the end, all they exchanged were heated words, not hot lead. But Biggie could see how the situation had deteriorated.

He told *Vibe* that he looked Tupac squarely in the face, dead in the eyes for the first time since his hospitalization. The simmering rage he saw made him suspect Tupac really was out for blood. "That's when I knew it was on," he told *Vibe*.

In May, Tupac lashed out again. He dropped a B-side called "Hit 'Em Up." On the track, he accused Puffy and Biggie of premeditating his attack in 1994, dissed Bad Boy, issued veiled threats, and committed his claims about Faith to vinyl for posterity. "I fucked your bitch, you fat muthafucker. . . ." he rapped. Even hardcore hip-hop fans were stunned at the vicious intent of the cut.

Puffy couldn't imagine a worse situation. Not only did he seriously think Tupac was crazy, but he had an army of followers who would back him up. Puffy and Biggie had suddenly found themselves on one side of a nationwide war, and they didn't even have ammunition . . . because they'd never planned on getting into such a conflict in the first place.

Puffy just kept his fingers crossed that when the smoke cleared, they'd all be okay, and Bad Boy would still be doing well. And for the record, he continued to assert that nobody associated with Bad Boy had ever harmed Tupac. They hadn't done anything to intentionally provoke the animosity, and now they had people accusing them of attempted murder and dissing them on records. Puffy claimed in *Vibe* that Shakur knew who the real culprits in the 1994 shooting were, and that he wouldn't confront the perpetrators because they'd come after him again. So instead he'd decided to make the main men of Bad Boy his scapegoats.

But Puffy said he forgave Tupac. At the end of the day, he insisted, Tupac Shakur was just a nice guy from New York who loved hip-hop, the same as he himself and Biggie.

All the media attention wasn't helping the situation, either. The fans picked up on it and drew sides. Artists capitalized on the conflict to generate attention around their new releases. The atmosphere was becoming increasingly chaotic, approaching a state of total entropy, where nothing positive could be accomplished.

Some argued that the label heads themselves were driving the conflict in order to increase record sales, and even Suge Knight hinted that the publicity wasn't hurting his business. But Puffy didn't see the gain in such dealings. As the head of a label that he wanted to see achieve global fame, alienating half the country seemed like a suicidal proposition. He was embarrassed at the very suggestion that he might stoop so low.

Through all the turmoil, Biggie never fought back. He never cut a record in which he responded to Tupac's vitriol. He barely even addressed the situation. When he did, he insisted that he'd never had a beef with his West Coast counterpart. He claimed he knew more about Tupac than people realized, about what made him behave as he did. He'd been there when Tupac had bought his first Rolex, back when Biggie wasn't making enough dough to afford such luxuries. Biggie would intimate that Tupac learned much from him in their time together, yet had still chosen to make unfortunate choices about the company he kept and the activities he engaged in. Yet regardless of the reasons he'd turned on his former friend, the big man knew that in the deepest recesses of his heart, Tupac couldn't deny the kinship they'd felt. Biggie admitted in *Vibe* that he couldn't change the way Tupac felt now, "but it wasn't like he wasn't my man."

# 10

# A Time of Change

Mercifully, despite the situation between Bad Boy and Death Row, there were plenty of bright spots on Puffy's horizon throughout 1996, too.

In June, over eight hundred music-industry executives convened at Roseland in New York City for ASCAP's Rhythm and Soul Music Awards. Hosted by one of the industry's most prestigious and oldest organizations, the awards were a star-studded affair. Among the guests were KRS-One, Ashford & Simpson, Frankie Knuckles, and Uptown alumni Andre Harrell and Heavy D, plus Bad Boy family members Craig Mack and Faith Evans.

Puffy and Biggie were awarded the honors for Top Rap Song for "One More Chance/Stay with Me" (they shared the prize with Bunny and Mark DeBarge, composers of "Stay with Me"). But more significantly, Puffy was singled out for the distinction Songwriter of the Year.

The number of hit records he'd written or cowritten in the previous year was stunning: "Can't You See" for Total, "Be Happy" for Mary J. Blige, "One More Chance" with B.I.G., "You Used to Love Me" for Faith.

"We are honoring exceptional talents this evening," said ASCAP president and chairman Marilyn Bergman. In Puffy's case, that was an understatement.

### The Men of 112

Also in the house that night were the newest members of the Bad Boy family, the all-male R&B vocal quartet 112. Composed of Daron Jones, Marvin, Mike, and Q, the group hailed from Atlanta, Georgia.

Originally members of the tenor section in the choir at Atlanta's Walter Franklin George High, the foursome became a group simply through an act of fate, when a teacher hand-picked each of them to sing together at a school function. "Afterwards somebody asked us to do a talent show," explained Q.

That second performance caught the attention of Courtney Stills and Kevin Wales, who quickly offered to manage them. They in turn introduced the four lads to Puffy, who was duly impressed with their smooth harmonies.

Puffy envisioned them as bridging the territory between Jodeci and Boyz II Men. With two sixteen-year-old members, and two who were seventeen, all male, they even mirrored the lineup of those established kingpins.

Displaying his usual degree of involvement from the word go, Puffy even picked the band's name, which already belonged to a regional hot spot known throughout Atlanta. The club 112 had been going strong for years, and Puffy wanted the band to have the same cachet with the players that frequented 112 and other establishments like it.

112, the group, was inspired primarily by their faith. Mike added that, like most of the Bad Boy artists, they felt a strong connection to God. "The church is a significant part of our lives."

So was the music they heard there. "We've modeled ourselves after Take 6, The Winans, and most of all, the gospel group Commissioned," Daron told *Essence*.

But the men of 112 also had an appreciation for secular music, and expressed their fondness for Babyface, Stevie Wonder, and Brian McKnight. Their eponymous debut album was distinguished by themes of love, both returned and rejected. Daron said they wanted their songs to tell stories, and characterized their compositions as "tasteful, not vulgar."

Puffy brought out the big guns for their album: Wayne Morris (of Boyz II Men), Al B. Sure!, and the Notorious B.I.G. The group members were ecstatic to have a chance to collaborate with some of their favorite performers on their debut. Not that the four tenors needed too much assistance; formidable songwriters as well as singers, they also penned hits for New Edition, Tevin Campbell, Gina Thompson, and Soul for Real.

Their album's standout track was the first single, "Only You," an up-tempo R&B number written by the band. With Stevie J and Puffy handling production, it quickly went platinum. But music lovers and industry insiders who really kept their eye on the prize were infatuated with a special guest Puffy slated for inclusion on the remix, an up-and-coming new rapper named Mase.

## Smooth as Mase

Puffy had stumbled upon Mase earlier in the year at the Gavin Music Seminar in Atlanta. The rapper, who was then working under the handle Mase Murder, had trekked down to Georgia from the Big Apple with some friends. His plan was to hunt down Jermaine Dupri, corner the producer, and lay some rhymes on him. And at a party Dupri was throwing at the Hard Rock Café, Mase got a chance to show off his stuff. Puffy asked Da Brat to take a breather during her set and let the unknown upstart try to rock the party. After hearing Mase on the mic, the Bad Boy CEO advised him to visit their offices as soon as he returned to New York.

Suddenly the undiscovered talent was a hot property. By the time he returned to New York, everybody knew he was about to join Bad Boy. Offers for two and three times what Puffy offered him rolled in, but in his heart, Mase knew there was only one choice.

Puffy and Mase had much in common. The young rapper had been born Mason Betha in Jacksonville, Florida. Like Sean Combs and Christopher Wallace, he had been raised by a single mother. His mom was employed by a public-housing agency. He never met his biological father.

His family migrated to New York when he was five. He'd grown up in Harlem: 139th Street and Lenox Avenue, to be exact. And just like his Bad Boy mentor, Mase felt the neighborhood had been an essential influence on his style. "Until I started playing basketball, and then later rapping, the streets of Harlem was the only world I knew," he told *Request* years later. The 'hood stayed in his heart wherever he might roam.

New York kids made fun of Mason's lackadaisical drawl. They'd tell the youngster that he sounded like he was mentally retarded when he spoke. "But as I got older the females would say my voice was sexy," he recounted in *The Source*.

Betha enjoyed attending school, and rarely

strayed from his studies. Around the neighborhood, folks took note of his studiousness and held high expectations for him. He reminisced in *The Source* that he had been the first person from his block to attend college.

He'd started out rhyming while still attending high school at the Manhattan Center for Science and Mathematics. He'd grown up among more established rappers, like Big L and McGruff, and sometimes even Jay-Z would come around. These were his primary sources of inspiration, and after listening to them, he began to formulate his own distinctive style of delivery.

After graduation, he attended the State University of New York at Purchase on an athletic scholarship. He had dreams of entering the NBA. "I wanted to be a pro, but it just ain't work out like that," he revealed in *Rolling Stone*. He was earmarked for a different destiny. After meeting Puffy his sophomore year, he decided to drop out and pursue performing full-time.

His mother was less than enthusiastic about his career choice. He admitted in *Rolling Stone* that she'd been very disappointed when he quit school for music. "But she always respected my decisions, and I just told her that this is my dream."

For a spell, Mase hooked up with another Harlem outfit, The Lox. He'd met members Jadakiss, Sheek, and Styles one afternoon on

125th Street, where the trio was taking on any challengers who could beat their rhymes.

Jadakiss recalled in *The Source* that they were just freestyling, taking on all comers and systematically reducing them to dust with their lyrical skills. Then their manager's brother skipped off for a moment, returning with a young challenger: Mase. He was the only contender who could keep up with them, and the nicest in the whole bunch, too. As the old adage says, if you can't beat 'em, join 'em. "So we brought him into the farm."

But Puffy thought Jadakiss and Mase sounded too much alike, and advised them to split so each could develop independently. No matter; they both ended up signed to Bad Boy.

From the moment Mase laid down his lyrics on the "Only You" remix, ears began perking up. His voice was fresh and unique, his style unusual but accessible. "You can't put a finger on him," observed Bad Boy A&R guy and producer Deric "D-dot" Angelettie (part of Puffy's elite production squad, the Hitmen) in *Rolling Stone*. He sounded neither young nor old, neither hard nor soft. He wasn't a gangsta, but you could hear the streets in his delivery.

And he wasn't trying to be anything he wasn't. "It's not really about talent," Mase said in *Rolling Stone* of his unconventional style. His rapping was simply an extension of his everyday speech. This was how he spoke first thing in the morning, in interviews or business meetings. Even when people tried to make him angry, his voice remained laid-back and smooth.

He was a perfect foil for Puffy, because he could appreciate how demanding the producer could be, and why it was important. "In the studio, Puff is like a coach trying to bring out the best in his players," Mase observed in *Request*. Practice might be grueling, but the strain would be worth it once the team won the championships.

## Tragedy for Tupac

On September 7, 1996, Tupac Shakur and Suge Knight were in Las Vegas. Accompanied by members of their crew, the two Death Row giants had made the trip to Sin City to watch heavyweights Mike Tyson and Bruce Seldon fight at the MGM Grand Hotel and Casino. Unfortunately, the fight didn't last very long; Tyson tore his foe apart in less than two minutes, sending spectators back into the night.

On the way to pick up their cars, Tupac had gotten into a scuffle with an unidentified black man (who later turned out to be one Orlando Anderson, of Compton, California) in the casino. Hotel security broke it up, and the group continued on.

Tupac was staying at another hotel, The Luxor, with his girlfriend. The Death Row entourage stopped long enough for him to change clothes. Feeling reasonably confident that he didn't need to worry about L.A.-style gang violence in the Nevada resort town, Tupac was neither carrying a gun nor wearing a bulletproof jacket. Besides, in the desert heat, such heavy protection was decidedly uncomfortable.

After making another stop for drinks at Suge Knight's local pad, the Death Row convoy, consisting of approximately ten cars, headed out for a benefit party at nearby Club 662. With Tupac riding shotgun, Suge drove his BMW to the joint. Heavy Saturday-night traffic on Vegas's main drag, known to locals as "The Strip," delayed their progress. At one point they were detained momentarily by the police, for playing their music too loud and not having proper tags on the car. But after a couple questions, the cops let the duo continue.

They paused at an intersection, with members of their group in vehicles behind them and to their left. Suddenly a light-colored Cadillac slid into position on the right side of the BMW. An unidentified gunman in the back fired at least thirteen rounds of ammunition from a high-powered semiautomatic handgun into the passenger side of Knight's car.

Tupac was hit four times. The assailants peeled out and managed to escape, although several cars gave chase. Suge Knight, who had also been hit by a single bullet, immediately discerned that Shakur was seriously injured. Although his car now had two flat tires, he attempted to pull out and search for medical assistance. In the confusion and congestion, they didn't get far, but help reached them quickly. Both men were taken for treatment at University Medical Center, Las Vegas's county hospital.

Knight's minor head wound was treated and he was placed in a normal hospital room. But Tupac's condition was serious. He was rushed to the trauma unit and underwent emergency surgery. Over the course of the following week, as hip-hop fans waited in stunned silence, Shakur's condition remained highly unstable. He had suffered a severe chest wound, and his chances of survival were not good.

Six days after the attack, on Friday, September 13, 1996, Tupac Shakur died. Despite a tremendous amount of speculation in law-enforcement circles, the music world, and particularly the media, the murder would remain unsolved.

Given the climate between the Bad Boy and Death Row camps, there were plenty of whispered allegations that Puffy, Biggie, or someone close to them had been involved in the murder. The men at Bad Boy couldn't believe something this terrible had happened to Tupac. They were shocked and hurt.

But knowing the ways of the media all too

well, they soon grew afraid, and tried to brace themselves for the inevitable. It seemed to Puffy as if their pictures appeared in every early report that ran in Los Angeles or Las Vegas. This only escalated the finger-pointing and provoked people to speculate further about a dispute the Bad Boy family had struggled so hard to downplay.

But Puffy told *Time* there was zero percent truth to speculation that he, or anyone close to him, had been involved in the tragedy. He claimed he could never have somebody murdered—that nobody deserved such a horrible fate, being gunned down in the street. The conflict between Bad Boy and Death Row hadn't been a matter of life and death. "Our problems were some record company–type shit."

Biggie later concurred in *Spin* that he'd had absolutely nothing to do with Tupac's murder. Death wasn't an end he'd wish on anybody. He reiterated how much he'd respected Tupac's skill as a rapper, and how sorry he was to see him gone.

Puffy tried to make people understand that he'd never played into the East Coast vs. West Coast brouhaha. It was all a gross misunderstanding as far as he was concerned. "I don't think you can be in a feud with somebody if there's not two people arguing," he insisted in *USA Today*. He claimed he'd never had a bone to pick with Tupac, Suge Knight, or Death Row.

"The only thing I've heard is the records that you've heard," he said, alluding to the various insults lobbed between coasts on tracks by various rappers. He'd never been aware of the conflict on any other level. "So it was more hype than anything."

## Controlling His Destiny

A few weeks later Puffy was back in the news again, but this time for positive reasons. In just three years Bad Boy Entertainment had sold twelve million CDs, records, and cassettes. When it came time to negotiate a new deal with their parent company, Arista Records, Puffy and company played hardball. The Bad Boy CEO had once remarked that when black businessmen baked a pie with their successes, the music industry let them keep only the crust. He was determined to play an increasingly important role around the bakery.

Although the specifics of the deal were kept secret, industry sources claimed the new five-year pact included a credit line up to $70 million for Bad Boy, plus an advance of over $5 million. To sweeten the deal, a new studio for Puffy, the aptly named Daddy's House, was also thrown in. Most important, Bad Boy Entertainment would now become a joint venture, meaning Arista would share ownership fifty-fifty with Puffy.

## A Time of Change

The negotiations hadn't gone smoothly. At one point while talks were stalled, Puffy had even shut down the label for a brief spell. He took a vacation in Trinidad and entertained overtures from other interested parties. Meanwhile, the news of Tupac's death and the state of the hip-hop nation had Arista executives worried; rumors claimed they'd even examined the life-insurance provisions in Puffy's contracts. But in the end the deal was sealed.

Puffy wouldn't elaborate on the details for the press, but simply said in *Newsweek* that with the new agreement, "I control my own destiny." And now he'd almost certainly have the right to buy Arista's share of Bad Boy in five years; such rights are normal for joint ventures. By 2001, Sean "Puffy" Combs might be the first hip-hop label mogul on a par with David Geffen.

Amid the turmoil, Biggie was completing the follow-up to *Ready to Die*. Months earlier he'd announced the title: *Life After Death*. He planned to drop an epic record that recounted all his adventures, from Bed-Stuy to his million-selling status, and right on into the future. But what he didn't intend to do was consciously foster any further hatred between the East and West.

Puffy said later that Biggie hadn't wanted to make a record that would further exacerbate the volatile situation. He only wanted things to improve. Tupac had defamed Biggie's wife and his rapping skills—on wax, no less—and yet Biggie still turned the other cheek and remained silent.

No doubt about it, Biggie was still a formidable figure. He was tough and resilient. These qualities had already carried him through much in his short life, right up to the conflict with Tupac. But he wasn't headstrong or reckless like some of his peers, according to Puffy. He was tough in the right way. Everyone at Bad Boy was ready for *Life After Death* to wipe the slate clean.

Still, there had been perceptible changes in Biggie's personality that came with his success, and the new material reflected that. On *Ready to Die*, he'd been telling intensely personal stories; the music was secondary at times. He'd had stories to tell, but sculpting the musical tracks into unified soundscapes hadn't always commanded his full attention. But on *Life After Death*, he found more pleasure in creating the actual music.

He'd also gone through some other changes, and matured. He and Faith had had a son, Christopher, Jr., and his daughter T'Yanna (from an earlier relationship) was growing up. No matter how he and his wife might fight, he enjoyed his children, and his family life, a lot more. He'd grown as a human being.

But as Puffy observed on *MTV News*, the whole Bad Boy family was growing up together. They'd been blessed with the chance to enjoy such great success while they were still very young, but they had much to learn, and were maturing every day. "We're still making mistakes," he admitted.

But worrying about learning the hard way wasn't about to stop Puffy from finally realizing one of his own dreams. For years he'd been appearing in other artists' videos and rapping on their tracks. He'd written, produced, and remixed dozens of hits. It was time for him to finally step into the spotlight as a performer. By November of 1996, word in the papers was that the full-length recording debut of Puff Daddy, featuring cameos from most of the extended Bad Boy family, would be dropping in early '97.

"I was just having fun, makin' hot records," he would say in *Spin* of the tracks he laid down for the album tentatively entitled *Hell Up in Harlem*. "The concept was to have fifteen hits on it."

He'd been watching his stars and their peers bring down the house with their performances for years, and he wanted his chance to shine. For detractors who had long grumbled about Puffy's larger-than-life personality, this was just another affront to the underground. But it didn't matter to him how absurd anyone else thought his dream was. He confessed to *The Source* that he lived in fear of turning forty one day and regretting that he'd never tried to be a performer. "I never want to hear myself say that."

# 11

## A Death in the Family

As 1996 wrapped up and the New Year began, Puffy upped the ante and released "Can't Nobody Hold Me Down," his debut single as a solo artist, with some added assistance from Mase. Although he had recently hit the pop charts as a featured artist alongside Lil' Kim on her hit "No Time," this was the first time a record had borne the name Puff Daddy as the main attraction.

A teaser from the forthcoming *Hell Up in Harlem*, "Can't Nobody Hold Me Down" was a classic example of Puffy's gift for borrowing and reinterpreting songs from the not-so-distant past. The title for his track was lifted from a 1984 Top 5 single entitled "Break My Stride," originally released by Matthew Wilder (a New York–based singer/songwriter who'd worked with Bette Midler and Rickie Lee Jones).

The recognizable musical hook came from

the same era, but the opposite end of the radio dial. It was appropriated from "The Message," a 1982 tune from Grandmaster Flash and the Furious Five. The original cut had climbed to number four on the R&B charts (it peaked at number sixty-two pop, impressive for the time). And with its unwavering depiction of ghetto street life, "The Message" had signaled a shift in the direction rap music was taking—away from lighthearted party music and toward social commentary.

Puff Daddy's track was intended to serve as a warning to detractors who claimed he was overexposed or too commercial. Naturally, his incorporation of a sample from a record with important political significance for the hip-hop community rubbed some people the wrong way. But Puffy was not fazed.

He felt that the message of "Can't Nobody Hold Me Down" dovetailed neatly with the intention behind "The Message." He claimed his tune also had a similar message. It was one that had been part of songs he'd previously written and produced for other artists, and one that kids needed to hear now more than ever: That no matter what obstacles stood in your way, you could achieve success.

Besides, Grandmaster Flash (Joseph Saddler) had already given Puff Daddy the nod of approval. The two already knew each other from the scene, and the elder statesman was complimentary about the song. "Flash loved it and he was proud of it and I thank him," said Puffy on MTV.

The originators of hip-hop had opened a creative door for urban youth to step through and find success. Puffy appreciated that his rewards had come as a direct result of their hard work. He was proud to be a part of that legacy, and felt that those who had come before him appreciated the unique progress he and the Bad Boy posse had continued to make in their own fashion.

Besides pushing his Puff Daddy persona even further into the mainstream, Combs also used "Can't Nobody Hold Me Down" to generate more excitement about his new protégé Mase.

Although Mase's own album, *Harlem World,* was still being recorded at the time, he agreed with Puffy's decision to unleash "Can't Nobody Hold Me Down" as soon as possible. He knew it was a bad idea to sit on the track until he had his own product to back it up. That might take too long, and compromise the success of Puffy's song.

This didn't mean that Puffy wasn't putting special care into Mase's debut set. "The reason the album took so long to record is because Puff wants everything perfect," Mase admitted to *Request.*

But even though Mase would become a hit on both the song and the accompanying video for "Can't Nobody Hold Me Down," his initial reaction to the finished track was negative (as it had purportedly been on 112's "Only You" remix). In particular, he didn't feel comfortable with the beat. Puffy told him not to worry, that the premiere Puff Daddy single would connect with the fans.

As usual, Puffy's instincts were correct. Mase had believed the track would eventually break, but only after a slow build. But it was huge almost from the day of release. Within nine weeks of first appearing, on March 22, "Can't Nobody Hold Me Down" would ascend to the number-one position on the Hot 100 chart. Bad Boy Entertainment's first number-one record was also the crowning moment to date for the label's talented and visionary CEO. But the fruits of Puff Daddy's success were going to prove bittersweet. . . .

## The Darkest Hour

Late in February 1997, Biggie headed out to Los Angeles to do promotion for his hotly anticipated second album *Life After Death*, scheduled for release on March 25. He was hanging out in the sunshine and enjoying life, and rehearsing for MTV's *Spring Break*. He was also shooting a video for his next single, "Hypnotize." As Puffy observed, if Biggie deserved only the best, it simply made more sense to film the clip in Hollywood. After all, that's where movies are made.

Biggie did plenty of radio and magazine interviews during this spell, too. He was determined to show people he'd come to California in peace, to eliminate any further animosity. He was going to seize every opportunity afforded him to defuse the so-called East Coast/West Coast rivalry. He'd even written a new cut, "Goin' Back to Cali," to show the people of the left coast that he bore them no ill will.

Puffy joined him on the West Coast junket. Although both men wanted the feud to end, they had beefed up their security for the visit. In light of all the tensions stoked by ceaseless media attention, it seemed a wise precaution.

The weekend of March 7, both men were scheduled to appear on the eleventh annual Soul Train Music Awards. On nationwide television, the duo presented an award to Toni Braxton.

The next evening, Saturday, March 8, they decided to attend a party at the Peterson Automotive Museum on Wilshire Boulevard. The event was hosted by Tanqueray spirits, *Vibe* magazine, and Qwest Records (the label owned by one of Puffy's idols, producer Quincy Jones). Although the evening would assuredly be star-studded, the pair felt the atmosphere would be fairly comfortable. After all, it was technically a private party.

## A Death in the Family

Biggie had originally been scheduled to go into the studio that day, but he didn't feel like it. *Life After Death* was finally wrapped up, and the rapper just felt like having some fun. He wanted to go out and celebrate with his best friend. Biggie was contemplating an acting career, and hoped he could network with some Hollywood hustlers. Puffy was pleased to see his star attraction looking for new opportunities to challenge his abilities.

But because Biggie had broken his leg shortly before, he was using a cane and couldn't walk around or dance. Typically, the hyperactive Puffy wouldn't sit still for long at such a function. But Biggie wanted to hang with his friend, and asked the producer to just camp out at a table with him all night. Puffy agreed. So they chilled out and enjoyed themselves, drinking and listening to the music, never leaving the table.

Stars like Russell Simmons, actor Wesley Snipes, and singer Seal were all in the house. Friends and colleagues dropped by to say hello and wish them well. Sitting in a room filled with the A-list of the Young, Black, and Fabulous, listening to their own records played alongside the hits of their peers, the pair felt a sense of pride. That only increased when a Bad Boy song would drop and folks got busy on the dance floor. After all, that was why the two made music in the first place.

Biggie was in a good mood. He felt confident about the record he'd completed, and that the rivalry that had shadowed his life for the past two years plus was about to end. He mentioned to Puffy how excited he was in particular for West Coast playas to hear "Goin' Back to Cali" so they'd realize he'd never hated them.

Eventually, the party became too crowded. The fire marshals showed up to shut the joint down. With Biggie's broken leg, it took the fellas a little while to maneuver their way out into the early morning. They waited outside for a few minutes, and just continued talking about the usual: music, the party, girls. The cars pulled around. Puffy and some of their entourage climbed into the first of two rented GMC Suburbans; the rest of the crew, including Biggie and his driver, D-Rock, piled into the second. A Chevy Blazer with a security escort of hired off-duty police officers followed directly behind the two.

The convoy pulled out of the parking lot, then made a right turn onto Fairfax Avenue. As all three cars came to a halt for a red light at the intersection at Wilshire Boulevard, a dark-colored car pulled up alongside Biggie's vehicle. A moment later, as the Bad Boy cars began to pull out, the driver of the unidentified automobile aimed a nine-millimeter gun out the window and opened fire on the rapper's Suburban, firing between six and ten shots.

As they crossed through the light Puffy heard gunshots ring out. He ducked down to safety.

154

# A Death in the Family

For a minute he thought perhaps somebody at the party was showing off. It wouldn't be the first time he'd attended a joint where some fool started firing a gun into the air to create a stir.

But then somebody looked back and yelled that Biggie's car had been hit. Puffy threw open the door—while his own car was still moving—and ran to help his friend. Because if Biggie had been hit by a bullet, or the assailants planned to hit the car again, the rapper was trapped. He couldn't leave the vehicle because of his injured leg.

Puffy dashed back to Biggie's Suburban and found that everyone except D-Rock had already jumped out, fearing another round of gunfire. Biggie was slouched over in the passenger's seat.

Unable to extract his massive frame from the car, Puffy and D-Rock propped Biggie up in the seat. D-Rock slid back in behind the wheel, and Puffy leaped in back. They began speeding to Cedars-Sinai Medical Center, a few blocks away.

Puffy was speaking to Biggie, telling him to hold on. He began to pray frantically, telling his friend over and over not to let go, begging Biggie's spirit not to leave this mortal coil just yet. But his best friend wasn't answering, and Puffy feared the worst. He'd witnessed people's deaths before, and recognized the subtle vibrations that signaled the beginning of the end.

Finally, they reached the hospital. D-Rock and Puffy helped the emergency personnel hoist Biggie's body onto a stretcher.

Puffy spent the seemingly endless minutes that followed down on his knees, praying to God to spare his friend's life. But his pleas were in vain. Within half an hour a doctor had come to tell them the tragic truth. Twenty-four-year-old Christopher Wallace, the Notorious B.I.G., was dead.

Puffy, D-Rock, and the others were in shock. The driver—D-Rock—who shared a house with Biggie and Little Caesar in New Jersey, and had grown up with him, tried to call Voletta Wallace. But when he got Biggie's mother on the phone, he broke down. He couldn't tell her the horrible news. Somehow, Puffy found the strength. He tried to calm her down and find someone to go care for her in this dark hour.

Then he began to go into shock. An endless loop of prayers kept repeating in his mind as he beseeched God to somehow dispel the horrible tragedy he'd just seen played out before his eyes. "I was praying that I had got hit and I was in a coma and I was just dreaming," he told *Vibe*.

Unable to accept the events that had just transpired, Puffy began shutting down. Escorts brought him back to his hotel room. He wanted to sleep more than he could ever recall. If only he could fall asleep, perhaps it really would be nothing but a terrible dream when he awoke.

# A Death in the Family

News quickly reached Faith Evans that her husband had been shot. She also had been at the *Vibe* party that evening, and they had spoken briefly. Although relations between them had been strained, she still cared for her estranged husband deeply. They were both strong-willed and stubborn. Their last phone conversation had ended with them hanging up on each other.

But even if they hadn't been on the best of terms when he passed, that didn't mean the bond between them had been severed. There were still qualities that each sought out in the other, special needs that only they could fulfill for each other.

Although Faith knew there was nothing she could do, she felt the need to say good-bye to Biggie. "I just wanted to see him—whatever was wrong with him, however he looked—I just wanted to go in there and be with him," she recalled in *Essence*. But the hospital staff turned her away.

When Puffy woke up the next day, everyone around him was in a panic. Fearing for his life, they insisted he leave Los Angeles immediately. But Sean Combs was paralyzed. The thought of leaving his best friend behind overwhelmed him.

So great was his grief, he couldn't even find tears. Not yet. He went to the airport to fly back to New York. But when the plane pulled up to the gate, the horrible truth of what had happened came raining down on him. He realized he was leaving Los Angeles, without Biggie. His best friend, the man who'd helped him see his greatest dream come true, was lying dead in a morgue.

More than anything he'd ever wanted, Puffy wanted Biggie to be sitting in the seat next to him, returning to New York . . . going home. But this was one dream all the hard work in the world could never bring true.

### A Tribute to Biggie

Christopher Wallace, alias Biggie Smalls, alias the Notorious B.I.G., was buried on Tuesday, March 18. First, there was a private service and wake at an Upper East Side funeral home. Biggie had been laid out in a white suit and matching hat. Among the three hundred mourners were Mary J. Blige, Salt-N'-Pepa's Spinderella, Queen Latifah, and former New York City mayor David Dinkins. Faith sang at the service, and Puffy delivered the eulogy.

Puffy spoke of trying to come to grips with the loss of his friend. He recalled Biggie's good qualities. "What people need to know about B.I.G. is that he was compassionate, humorous, and generous," he said. But he pointed out that the rapper had been human, with his share of problems—problems like the ones all of America's urban black youth had to struggle with. With his music, B.I.G. had tried to reconcile the bitter truth of day-to-day ghetto life with the promise of creating a better life, or at least escaping the ugliness for a little while.

Puffy stressed that the music they made had never ever been intended to generate violence between the East and West Coast rap communities. And the animosity had to end. Too many lives had already been lost. It was time for the music to start healing, not hurting. As a gesture of his own commitment to moving forward, he promised to use Bad Boy profits to help Biggie's children grow up in the manner their father would have wanted.

"Christopher Wallace, aka Notorious B.I.G., you will always be in my prayers, along with all of the urban youth whose lives were ripped away by senseless violence," concluded Puffy. "It is time for a change."

Then the body began its journey home. As Biggie made one final trip back to Bed-Stuy, an estimated three thousand people waited in the vicinity of Fulton and St. James to welcome his funeral procession through the neighborhood.

The police were out, too, with helicopters and riot gear. But their presence only aggravated the atmosphere, and locals hollered at the authorities, as well as the reporters and photographers and cameramen from around the globe who swarmed his old Brooklyn stomping ground. Eventually, ten people would be arrested for disorderly conduct.

The devotion felt by Biggie's fans was evident from the sheer numbers who turned up to say good-bye. People also remembered Biggie's sense of style, and the dignity with which he carried himself, and dressed to the nines for the final farewell. Robert Marriott described the scene in *Ego Trip* magazine: "Braids of all kinds, fades, perms and waves, wraps, cornrows and camouflage, gold rings and leathers, scars and babies."

When the caravan finally wended its way round the bend, the mood altered. As the flower-covered hearse displaying the letters B.I.G. in red roses passed, a cheer and movement began. The Junior M.A.F.I.A. hung out of their limo windows, raising their hands and waving funeral programs. Lil' Kim sat in her car, crying ceaselessly. When the caravan hit the corner, the first refrains of Biggie's single "Hypnotize" pumped through the limo's car speakers, moving the hundreds of mourners. "For about thirty minutes," wrote Marriott, "all of Bed-Stuy convulsed in Biggie's rhythms."

Once again, as after the CCNY basketball disaster in 1991, Puffy sank into a deep depression. He didn't contemplate suicide, but he kept wondering why he couldn't have died so Biggie might have lived. And as before, he turned to his faith for solace. His belief in God was one thing he could always count on, and he prayed that the Lord would point him toward remedies for his pain. More than ever, he leaned on the church to help him find some shred of solace and a sense of perspective.

The absence of Biggie Smalls left a hole in Puffy's life that a man ten times B.I.G.'s stature would never fill. He lamented in *Vibe* that they hadn't spent enough time together just being friends. No matter how close they'd been, it had always seemed like they were working. Now they'd never have another chance to go on a vacation together or even just chill in each other's homes.

Puffy also looked to Biggie's family for comfort and strength. Voletta, Faith, and Biggie's two children all served as sources of encouragement to him. In particular, he admired Mrs. Wallace, and the strength that she seemed to draw from her ties to the church. He was grateful that she and Biggie had been close when he passed, and that she was looking after her grandchildren in this time of great loss. And if she could get up in the morning and go to work, face the world even though it had taken her only son from her, then Puffy would go on living and fighting, too.

Puffy vowed that he would do everything in his power to make sure that everyone Biggie had cared about was looked after to the best of his ability.

Meanwhile, even though they had been split

up at the time of his death, the responsibilities of Biggie's estate fell on Faith's small but powerful frame. She had to contend with the knowledge that Christopher, Jr., would never know his father.

Plus, there were debts to be settled, and people who owed Biggie money who didn't want to pay up now that the rapper was gone. Biggie didn't leave a will, so even though he and Faith were not living together, she inherited his entire estate. She split it all right down the middle with Voletta Wallace, although she wasn't legally obliged to. She knew it was the right thing to do.

The death of the Notorious B.I.G. threatened to eclipse everything wonderful that had already come to Puffy, and the rewards that still waited for him.

He was used to talking to his friend every day, laughing with him. The entire fabric of his life had been rent. His best friend no longer called him in the morning, or shared his dreams with him. Puffy's mind wouldn't let him think of anything else but Biggie's absence. He kept going over the events in his head again and again. He knew he was going in circles, that he wasn't moving forward, but didn't know how to stop.

There was one thing he was certain of, however: He'd come too far to quit now.

# 12

## I'll Be Missing You

The release of the Notorious B.I.G.'s *Life After Death* went ahead as scheduled. In wake of the tragic loss of Biggie Smalls, the album shot to number one on the *Billboard* 200, and would remain in the Top 100 for the duration of 1997.

The album's cameos from Bone Thugs n' Harmony, R. Kelly, and Lil' Kim met with applause, but—in death as in life—nobody stole the spotlight from the main attractions: the Notorious B.I.G. and Sean "Puffy" Combs. "Together they constructed a sprawling, cinematic saga of the thug life, a conscious continuation of *Ready to Die*," wrote Anthony DeCurtis of the modern masterpiece in *Rolling Stone*.

"Biggie already was somebody, and it's a sad but familiar irony that his senseless death has made him an even bigger star," observed Amy Linden in *People*. "His last recording is a series of cautionary tales that are offensive, exciting, disturbing, funky, and undeniably the product of a serious talent."

Eight weeks after his murder, on May 3, Biggie's first posthumous single, "Hypnotize," became the number-one song in the country. It was only the fifth time in the rock-and-roll era that a deceased performer had achieved the top slot, placing B.I.G. alongside John Lennon, Otis Redding, Janis Joplin, and Jim Croce in the annals of musical history. In his lifetime, the highest Biggie had ever seen one of his own tracks climb was number two, with "One More Chance/Stay with Me" back in the summer of 1995.

Following hot on the heels of "Can't Nobody Hold Me Down," "Hypnotize" was also the second Puffy-produced single (and Bad Boy Entertainment release) in a row to hit number one. The triumph was bittersweet.

Although younger fans were less likely to recognize it, the familiar sound of "Hypnotize" came courtesy of famous trumpet player Herb Alpert (who, ironically, was also a performer and label executive; the *A* in A&M Records stood for "Alpert"). "Hypnotize" borrowed from Alpert's late-seventies number-one instrumental hit "Rise."

The performer's nephew Randy Alpert, who cowrote the original, noted in *Billboard* how impressive it was that this riff had been a hit again. The music lovers who'd championed "Rise" in 1979 were now parents, with children who were digging a new hip-hop cut featuring the same musical materials. Puffy had bridged the generation gap with the track, a pattern he would become increasingly acclaimed for in the months to follow.

A week and a half after "Hypnotize" topped the charts, the nation paid homage to Biggie yet again. At noon on Wednesday, May 14, over two hundred radio stations honored him with a special tribute: a moment of silence. The thirty-second pause of radio silence (known as "dead air" in broadcasting parlance) was preceded by the debut of two new Bad Boy singles.

The first of the two fresh tracks had actually inspired the second. "We'll Always Love Big Poppa" by The Lox had taken shape in the weeks after Biggie's murder. When Puffy learned of it, he had a small epiphany. He had to write and record a tribute song of his own to help him come to terms with his loss.

Puffy's own offering to his fallen friend was entitled "I'll Be Missing You," and featured Biggie's widow, Faith (who also helped write it), as well as backing vocals by 112. The inspiration for the song had come from the classic Police song "Every Breath You Take," which had been a number-one hit for eight weeks in the summer of 1983. Although many people thought it had been written as a love song,

165

Sting insisted the original intention had been double-edged, with a sinister bent. During the record's heyday, he revealed it was all about "surveillance and ownership and jealousy," and characterized it as a fairly negative song.

But that wasn't how Puffy perceived it at all. "That's always been one of my favorite songs," he revealed in *Billboard*. "It's always made me cry." He said it evoked favorable memories of his father, Melvin Combs.

The inspiration for Puffy's tribute track had come in the weeks immediately following the murder, when he was bereft and disconsolate. One afternoon, he was watching MTV around the house, and the video for the Police chestnut came on. "It was like Biggie talking to me," said Puffy in *Vox*. The fact that MTV had chosen to broadcast such an old clip in the middle of the day seemed a good omen. Maybe Puffy had something he needed to say back to Biggie.

Still, he admitted in *Spin* of his track, "It's a selfish song." He and Faith had wanted a chance to make their peace with Biggie through music.

Expressing their feelings in the studio had been a painful experience. At points during the recording, both of them became so distressed they had to leave the room.

MTV and BET joined in the radio tribute of May 14, airing the video for "I'll Be Missing You." The clip featured Faith clad in white, singing with a choir of children, while Puffy danced gracefully in honor of his fallen friend. Puffy told *Vibe* it was more than a mere performance. "I'm talking to him through my dance."

The song and video dominated the airwaves throughout the summer and into the fall. It remained number one for eleven weeks, three weeks longer than the Police song that inspired it. Although countless music fans missed Biggie, the song's extended life also owed much to the fact that its subject wasn't mentioned by name in the video or lyrics. "It didn't really specify that it was about Biggie," DJ Angie Martinez of Hot 97 noted in *Spin*, "so anybody who ever lost somebody could relate to it."

Considering the inescapable nature of "I'll Be Missing You," and the tremendous financial rewards it reaped (all of which Puffy intended to turn over to charity and Biggie's children), it comes as little surprise that some folks felt the need to put the song down. But many music fans were aghast when no less a personage than Janet Jackson questioned Puffy's motives.

She announced that "I'll Be Missing You" had stirred her cynicism. "How much pain is [Puffy] really in?" she inquired in the *Chicago Tribune*. The fact that Puffy's stardom had increased monumentally in the wake of his best friend's demise didn't sit well with her.

Was his grief really sincere? "Or is this his way of squashing the pain?" (Ironically, later in the year Janet would a release a hit single of her own, "Together Again," that paid homage to loved ones who passed away.)

Whether or not Janet's feelings about Puffy had anything to do with his campaign to produce part of her next album, *The Velvet Rope,* or his exclusion from that project, no one can say for certain. On MTV, Puffy bemoaned the fact that while Janet's production team Jimmy Jam and Terry Lewis had gotten a shot at working with Mary J. Blige, he couldn't get in one track with Janet.

Janet insisted that Puffy hadn't been invited because he didn't express interest until the album was completed. "He had asked me a few times," she admitted, saying she hadn't ruled out the possibility of working together in the future. "I'm probably the only one who hasn't worked with him."

It seemed as though her moment had most likely passed, however. "It was just a dream, a fantasy to one day work with Janet Jackson," Puffy said with a sigh for the MTV cameras. It seemed that he didn't want to do so anymore, believing there were plenty of other fish in the sea. "My heart has been broken and I am moving on."

Besides, he didn't need to hitch his wagon to Janet Jackson's star to see the heavens. "I'll Be Missing You" would take him as far as any record conceivably could. It was number one on six different *Billboard* charts for eight consecutive weeks, and remained number one for eleven uninterrupted weeks on the pop singles chart. Transcending borders of language and culture, it also peaked at number one in fifteen other countries: the UK, Germany, Austria, Australia, Belgium, Canada, Denmark, Greece, Holland, Italy, Norway, Spain, Sweden, Switzerland, and New Zealand.

## Puff Daddy's Debut

On July 22, 1997, Puff Daddy released his debut full-length album as a performing artist. *No Way Out,* by Puff Daddy and the Family, sold over 560,000 copies in its first week on sale, making it the number-one album in the country.

Just before midnight the evening before the release, an estimated three thousand fans waiting to purchase copies of *No Way Out* created gridlock at the mammoth Virgin Megastore in Times Square of New York City. According to a Bad Boy press release, "The crowd packed into any available space in front of, across from, and surrounding the store."

The next day, July 23, Puffy and Mase took time out to give a show for hundreds of underprivileged kids at the Caramel Education Center for the Daddy's House Summer Camp.

Situated in upstate New York, the camp was yet another one of Puffy's charitable undertakings. The free concert was an opportunity for Puffy to encourage young people to pursue their dreams, while simultaneously thanking them for supporting his music.

Including both of Puff Daddy's number-one hits, "Can't Nobody Hold Me Down" and "Missing You," *No Way Out* had undergone an overhaul since Puffy's first pronouncements about his plans to pursue a recording career. In fact, he had rerecorded a good half of the material after Biggie's death.

"It's more serious now than when I first got into it," he told *Spin* when asked about his decision to abandon the earlier *Hell Up in Harlem* title. Some days he woke up and didn't want to continue making music—as an artist, a producer, or even a label CEO! But he didn't feel like there was any other choice. This was what he did best, what he had been born to do.

"At times, I feel like I'm trapped inside of a movie starring me, but I'm not the director, and I don't know what the scene is, nothing," Puffy admitted. The specific inspiration for the new album title had sprung from his sleeping subconscious, taken from a nightmare in which Puffy kept screaming, "There's no way out for me!" When he woke up, he knew he had to do this album.

But returning to the studio after Biggie's

death had proven an enormous challenge. "I didn't really want to make music, and honestly, I didn't even want to be the president of this company [Bad Boy Entertainment]," he told Neil Strauss of *The New York Times*. But he and Biggie had built the Bad Boy empire together, and Puffy had accomplished too much to walk away from music entirely.

The content of *No Way Out* had been modified to reflect Puffy's current disposition. Instead of being nothing but party jams, it moved through an array of subjects and moods, from upbeat cuts to romantic numbers to reflective pieces that gave him a chance to express his feelings concerning Biggie's death. Songs like "If I Should Die Tonight" and "Is This the End?" were unflinching looks at the darker side of Puffy's party-hearty personality, while "Pain" addressed the early loss of his father and the way Puffy felt about the inexplicable hostility he seemed to inspire in some folks.

The album's supporting cast included Mase, Lil' Kim, Faith Evans, Foxy Brown, Busta Rhymes, 112, and The Lox. In some opinions, the involvement of Puff Daddy's extensive Family was the culmination of the popular hip-hop vogue for cross-pollination between artists, as exemplified on albums by supergroups like The Firm, or guest star–studded singles like Lil' Kim's "Not Tonight." (Another great example of such cooperation between artists came later in the year, when Puffy's

Rev. Run & the Christmas All Stars—featuring Mase, Puff Daddy, Snoop Doggy Dogg, Salt-N'-Pepa, Onyx, and Keith Murray—contributed the cut "Santa Baby" to the Special Olympics fund-raiser *A Very Special Christmas 3*.) The music world hadn't seen so many stars working together regularly since the golden era of jazz and blues clubs back in the forties and fifties, and more often than not it was Puffy bringing them together.

But the most significant presence throughout *No Way Out* was the specter of executive producer Biggie Smalls. His posthumous raps surfaced on several cuts, encouraging Puff and company to persevere and overcome. Not that there was any likelihood of Puffy ever forgetting his lost comrade.

"I miss him, but his presence is so strong," he admitted in *Essence*. He still spoke to Biggie. Even though the rapper wasn't there, Puffy knew he was listening.

"I'm a Biggie fanatic," he insisted. He even went so far as to have "B.I.G." tattooed on his body. "Remembering Biggie is never going to stop."

## Reinterpreting the Classics

In the newspapers and magazines, music critics came down hard on *No Way Out*. Some took exception with the dark themes permeating the album, most notably Puffy's understandable fixation with death on songs like "Pain" and "If I Should Die Tonight." Others dismissed his rapping as flat and monotonous, his rhymes uninspired.

Yet even though he didn't need to respond to his attackers—the support of his fans and colleagues was more than sufficient to sustain him—Puffy managed to consistently deflect or defend all these put-downs.

He contended that he was a lot better than plenty of people who billed themselves as rappers, but that he had too much respect for the art of rap to stake claims to that job description. The mark of a superlative rapper was his lyrical skills, and Puffy's vision was broader, more all-encompassing. He never insisted he was a dope MC; in fact, he thought of himself as an all-around entertainer. When he composed a track, he was simultaneously thinking about how the video would look, what choreography might complement the song onstage, how memorable the chorus was. Puffy was concerned with more than just rhyming—he wanted to control every detail of the whole glitzy package.

He cowrote his rhymes with the Family: Jay from The Lox, Lil' Kim, Jay-Z and so on. "I don't even try to touch Biggie's lyrical depth," he stressed in *Just for Black Men*. He hadn't grown up in the same environment as Biggie or Tupac, and wisely didn't attempt to comment on it. He wasn't a hard-core playa. His songs were aimed at breaking down the lingering racial divisions in popular music.

And nearly everyone in the press decried Puffy's dependence on samples from older songs for the basis of his own tracks.

Brett Ratner, who had been instrumental in crafting both Diana Ross's "I'm Coming Out" and David Bowie's "Let's Dance"—two tunes that had received the Puff Daddy treatment—commented in *Billboard*, "The sad thing is that in the year 2000, when the hot producer from that era samples Puffy, it's not gonna truly be Puffy's music he's sampling."

People came down on Puffy for his extensive use of samples, but often the records he built from them outsold the source material. And the folks he borrowed from weren't complaining about the royalties. "I make more money for the person than they made on the original," Puffy observed in British magazine *The Face*.

He had started sampling because he wanted to recapture the way certain records made him feel. But he didn't play any conventional instruments. He couldn't program drum machines or keyboards, but if he heard a record drop at a party and loved it, he wanted to figure out a way he could reinvent its magic and make it seem brand-new.

Sampling was an important element of hip-hop's legacy. But even Puffy was beginning to realize how heavily he leaned on it. He told *Spin* he'd actually decreased his use of samples on *No Way Out* as a consequence.

Not enough, however, to appease some hard-core fans. When a writer from *The Source* pressed the issue, Puffy almost lost his cool. "Yes, I sample records," he retorted. "Yes, I'm a beatjacker." He knew the practice rubbed some people the wrong way, but it got a hell of a lot more of them running for the dance floor. When a Puff Daddy record came on, people's booties started bouncing.

The pros and cons notwithstanding, Puffy's ability to co-opt older tunes was leading to opportunities to work with the original artists, like Sting and Diana Ross. He told *The Face* he was going to be producing new records for both of them, and Aretha Franklin was slated for a Puff Daddy makeover, too.

"There's a misconception that I have this big record collection," he said in *Rolling Stone*. In fact, he had never collected records as a youth. He didn't have a patented formula, or a master plan simply to pilfer the greatest hits of the seventies and eighties until he ran out. If you looked below the surface, there was more to a Puff Daddy production than a familiar sound byte and some rapping. It took a little more than a knack for recycling to keep churning out records that consistently sold multiple millions of copies.

Puffy felt confident that he had a unique knack for reinterpreting the classics, even ones that hadn't aged too well. Cyndi Lauper? No problem. Duran Duran? Say when. He laughed to *The Face* that he had met the British New Wave sensations at MTV not long ago. "They said they were fans."

In one sense, his decision to use this or that song was a nod to the gifts of the person behind it in the first place. "Been Around the World" used David Bowie's "Let's Dance" as a foundation, and Puffy was quick to admit that he admired both the UK superstar's work with artist/producer Nile Rodgers in the mid-eighties, but also his more recent forays into drum and bass. Puffy told *The Face* he admired Bowie and his pioneering role in popular music. "I think he's extremely creative and I respect him for that."

Given his background, he noted it made more sense for Puff Daddy to plunder the vaults of Top 40 radio than stick strictly to rap classics. "I was middle class growing up," he told *Time*. "I grew up with white kids and Chinese kids. I grew up listening to Ozzy Osbourne *and* 'Rapper's Delight.'"

Puffy claimed he knew so many hits from the eighties because he'd sat with his ear to the radio during his youth. He couldn't watch television as much as other children, because

176

his grandmother and mother used the revoking of TV privileges as a way to discipline him when he misbehaved. He said the radio had been his only source for pop culture, because other entertainment had been forbidden.

Puffy's eclectic tastes often surprised people. There was definitely more to his listening diet than hip-hop, and he named everyone from Cyndi Lauper to Radiohead in interviews. He was an unabashed Phil Collins fan. In fact, he could give anybody a hit record, if they wanted. Even Hootie & the Blowfish.

Puffy's business and musical moves only served to reinforce his lack of musical bias. He even signed a Los Angeles rock band called FuzzBubble to Bad Boy. He judged people by their drive, their desire to leave a mark on the world, irrespective of their sound. "I can do anything, I could do any type of music," he said to *The Face*.

Detractors who demanded proof of this boast needed to look no further than the flip side of the next single from *No Way Out*, "Been Around the World." For the two rock remixes of "It's All About the Benjamins," Puffy augmented his crew to include not only FuzzBubble, but also Rob Zombie of heavy-metal behemoth White Zombie, bassist Tommy Stinson (formerly of seminal Minneapolis punk act The Replacements) of Perfect, and—most impressively—Dave Grohl, of Nirvana and Foo Fighters renown.

Grohl confessed to *Vibe* that he'd been terrifically flattered when he received the invitation to participate. "I'd seen his videos on MTV, and he seemed like this way larger-than-life pop star, this bad ass." The Seattle grunge legend was even more impressed when Puffy showed up for the recording session . . . in his church clothes.

Grohl wasn't able, however, to take time out of his busy schedule to appear in a special video Puffy shot for the new version (even though he was in Los Angeles, where the video was shot, at the same time). No matter, the alternate version, which featured Puffy, Lil' Kim, and The Lox taking over the entertainment at a high-school prom, with some help from a yelping Stinson, was a huge hit. The clip even poked sly fun at R.E.M., starting with a lounge singer's rendition of their song "Everybody Hurts" that prompts Puffy and company to bust a move and get the party started right.

Like practically every other video he appeared in, the rock version of "It's All About the Benjamins" ignited MTV. Another video version of "Benjamins" saw Puffy square off against celebrated tap dancer Savion Glover for some very fancy footwork. As far as Glover (who'd recently won a Tony Award for his choreography for *Bring in Da Noise, Bring in*

*Da Funk*, the Broadway musical in which he starred) was concerned, the pairing made perfect sense. "Tap's foundation is jazz, just like hip-hop, so relating tap-dancing to rap is natural for me," he said. "When Puffy asked me to do the video, I said, yes. Cuz it's all about the Benjamins!"

Puffy held his own with the Broadway star, even though his formal dance training was minimal. "I'm just doing what my body feels," he said in *Jet*. He took much of his inspiration from the way James Brown, one of his idols (who would also approach Puffy to consider producing him), had moved in his prime. "He just did what his body felt. If you ever look at his dances, they looked a little bit awkward. They looked a little bit funny with his gyrating and moving his feet all quick."

Puffy had even purportedly taken time out to compose a track with critical favorite Beck ("Loser," "Where It's At"). The song had been considered for inclusion on *No Way Out*, but didn't fit in with the finished record. He admitted in *Just for Black Men* that the unusual collaboration was likely to surface on a soundtrack. The title of the tune seemed to suit their dynamic well; they'd called it "The Odd Couple," "because we're total opposites of each other."

Yet while many of the biggest names in entertainment continued lining up to work with

Puffy, Janet Jackson wasn't the only party who publicly admitted they weren't completely in awe of the producer-turned-performer. MTV radio networks announced that Nick Hexum of hip-hop/alternative hybrid act 311 turned down an offer to rap on a "Benjamins" remix.

Plus, with the talk in camp Bad Boy of sparkling Cristal and big cars, were Puffy and company still placing too much emphasis on material gain as a measure of success? Puffy professed in *Vibe* that he thought that most people believed he passed his days spending limitless loot, running on reckless shopping sprees. Or, conversely, that he devoted all his free time to running with street thugs. Perhaps fans imagined that he did nothing but make videos all day and cruise around in limousines from shoot to shoot. None of it was true.

The Bad Boy artists went in for flash and extravagance, but they made sacrifices, too. With such busy agendas and hectic schedules, they had minimal time for their private lives, and few opportunities to regroup and find some peace of mind.

And not everyone approved of Puff Daddy's status. "It ain't really fly to be successful in young Black America," he complained to *Essence*. "You're hated." He knew that countless folks thought he just spent his afternoons lounging around waiting for his close-up, or signing autographs, while the rest of the world toiled for minimum wage. And nothing he could do would convince some people otherwise, no matter how much he might do on behalf of worthy causes.

Few people could appreciate Puffy's position better than Sister Souljah, a controversial writer and rap artist who had been the subject of a media witch-hunt for her outspoken recordings. Admiring her commitment to improving community standards, Puffy had appointed her the executive director of Daddy's House Social Programs, Inc., his nonprofit organization working with New York–area youth.

Souljah noted that the biggest criticism she regularly heard of Puffy in hip-hop circles was that his sound was "too commercial." But in her experience, you'd be hard-pressed to find a recording artist who wasn't interested in making money. It struck her as highly hypocritical.

Puffy admitted that it troubled him to realize most people wouldn't genuinely appreciate what he'd done—as an artist, a businessman, or a humanitarian—until he was gone. At times loneliness threatened to overwhelm him, hurl him back into deep depression again. "I just break down and start crying—just to get it out of my system," he told *Essence*. Why did achieving so much have to come at the expense of being able to live normally?

## Young, Black, and Successful

"I've still got a long way to go to make the type of impact I want to make," Puffy insisted to UK music magazine *Vox*. The measure of success to him came from a different source than money; for Puffy, there was no greater rush than watching a party full of people go berserk when one of his records came on.

"I'm just here to make people dance, I ain't here for the critics," he reiterated in *The Face*. There were plenty of other artists and producers concentrating on giving voice to negativity or sadness in their songs. That didn't interest Puffy. Bringing people joy through music was his motivation.

The key to Puff Daddy's success, as an artist, producer, and label executive, lay in his ability to put aside the prejudices that hindered other music-industry hustlers, and use his eyes and ears to gauge exactly what the public wanted. He revealed to Veronica Webb in *Interview* that he was just as likely to draw on rock bands like Nirvana, Soundgarden, or Pearl Jam as the newest hip-hop artist. His mission was to incorporate all the different sounds people liked, "from a rebellious vibe to the vibe of crying out from hurt or happiness to just wanting to let go and party."

The other Bad Boy artists didn't have any trouble appreciating that approach. "He's giving you a lot of what you like," said Mase of the Puff Daddy style in the *Chicago Tribune*. When most fellas go for a haircut, they tell the barber exactly how they want the finished style to look. "But Puffy doesn't get it cut the way he likes," said Mase. "He'll go in there and say, 'Now, how would the ladies like me to cut it?' " He approached making records the same way. Pleasing music fans was his number-one priority, not making records just to entertain himself or a cadre of die-hard hip-hop purists.

Puffy confessed to *The Source* that there were many occasions when he'd collected awards for his work and looked out into the crowd and saw the brothers and sisters scowling at him. It hurt him to see other people criticize his success, even as he broke down barriers in the music community and beyond. But this had happened in the world of hip-hop before.

Like Puffy, eighties icon MC Hammer had made a mint building tracks around other artists' records and incorporating captivating dance routines into his videos. Likewise, he'd been savaged for diluting rap and bringing it to the mainstream with hit singles like "U Can't Touch This" and "2 Legit 2 Quit." Puffy identified with his predecessor. Puffy loved MC Hammer, and admired how he'd crossed lines of culture, geography, and class.

Puffy realized that his rise to prominence meant racial barriers were breaking down further in America as a direct result of the increasing popularity of hip-hop. He said in *Entertainment Weekly* that this was his dream come true: "I made my music for the urban community, but I want everybody to feel it." And he didn't want scandals or rivalries or animosity to interfere with that goal. He wanted to find solutions, not stir up more problems. Daddy's House and his other charities were his means for encouraging kids who did good in the world.

Time and again he stressed the importance of getting an education in his interviews, mentioning how much his spell at Howard had meant to him. Puffy gave 110 percent to try to make the world a better place for his young son Justin, and all children, to grow up in. He was tired of the nation's moral watchdogs making rap music a scapegoat for the problems of the young. He wanted people to admit their shortcomings, and confront the real roots of social and political troubles.

No matter how much money he made, Puffy insisted that neither he nor Biggie had ever been motivated solely by the Benjamins. He had fond memories of spying with Biggie on kids next to them in traffic from behind the limousine windows; nothing brought the duo greater satisfaction than to hear the kid's car system booming a Bad Boy jam. It made Puffy immeasurably happy to make other people enjoy themselves by listening to something he'd had a hand in creating.

Success might pay the bills, but Puffy struggled to keep his ego in check and stick to business, no matter how many records *No Way Out* sold. "I'm buggin' out," he admitted to Veronica Webb when she asked him what it felt like to finally have a hit album all his own. He'd never imagined the record could ever sell so many copies.

The artistic triumph of Puff Daddy wasn't going to distract Sean Combs from realizing all his dreams. He wasn't going to let fame affect him too much. He'd seen more than his share of ups and downs, and right now, with Puff Daddy mania running rampant, he was at a high point. But it might not last. He learned to savor the good times, because they flew away the fastest.

And underscoring that point, it seemed not a day went by that he didn't remind his fans and the media that he'd trade every record sold, every song of his on the radio, and every video on MTV, in exchange for one single thing: the return of his best friend, Biggie Smalls.

"I'm not getting over it," he said in *Essence*, describing the vacancy Biggie's absence had left in his life, in the fiber of his very being. "I'll never get over it." He didn't wish to appear ungrateful for all his blessings, but at the core, he wasn't completely content. He was better off financially than most, but that couldn't salve his emotional wounds. Only the return of Biggie could do that.

He swore to *Entertainment Weekly* that if Biggie coming back meant he could never make another hit record again, he'd be more than satisfied with that bargain. "Me and him could be mailmen," he said with a smile. "I'd be ecstatic with that."

# 13

## The High Price of Success

As 1997 continued to unfold, Sean "Puff Daddy" Combs was, without contest, the most visible figure in music and video. Every track he produced, every artist he squeezed into his schedule seemed to vault to the top of the R&B, hip-hop, and pop charts. MTV could easily have changed their moniker to PTV—Puffy Television—so ubiquitous were videos featuring Bad Boy artists and their extended family. The list was stunning: "I'm Still in Love with You/You Don't Have to Worry" by New Edition; "Cold Rock a Party" by MC Lyte; "You Should Be Mine (Don't Waste Your Time)" by Brian McKnight; as well as productions for Usher, Busta Rhymes, Lil' Kim, LL Cool J, and SWV.

With such a heavy schedule, it comes as no great revelation that Puffy doesn't sleep much. On the average, he gets about five hours of shut-eye a night. He usually wakes up around ten in the morning and immediately leaps on the phone. Around noon, he rises and heads out to inspect the status of his various projects, visiting the Bad Boy offices, and his Daddy's House recording studio. Later in the afternoon, he tends to interviews or rehearsals for upcoming appearances. Evenings are almost exclusively set aside for studio work, usually lasting into the wee hours of the morning, when he lays his head down for a few hours before starting the cycle all over again.

"And I love my job," he joked with *Rolling Stone*.

Unfortunately, not everyone in his life was as happy with his insatiable drive, no matter how much they respected his success. Janice Combs observed in *Vibe* that her son's meteoric rise was directly related to how seriously he took his work: "Sean is a workaholic." She worried that he didn't spend enough time resting and recuperating.

Even Puffy himself would confess on occasion that he wished there was a way to get off the merry-go-round from time to time, that his breakneck schedule brought him down. And he could see the impact it had on the people around him—his girlfriends, his mother, little Justin. But he admitted to *Vox* that work seemed to be all he knew how to do, even though he wanted to chill out sometimes.

He wished he could stop, but within a few minutes he was reaching for the phone again;

he even compared his need to network with an addiction. Even in the middle of the Sahara Desert, Puffy reckoned he'd be crawling over the burning sands to find a phone and make some business moves.

In light of his grueling schedule of events and appointments, the news that Bad Boy was being investigated for supposed links to street gangs involved in criminal activities (due largely to his position in the East/West feud and the subsequent deaths) seemed all the more ludicrous. Puffy was the president of the most successful custom label in America. Every moment when he wasn't on the go, he was in the recording studio producing someone. Unless he was suffering from multiple-personality disorder, it simply defied laws of physics for Puffy to be involved in "gangster stuff."

He moaned to Neil Strauss of *The New York Times* that summer that because of the way certain papers portrayed him, people thought of him as the black John Gotti, a powerful underworld figure using crime to protect his musical empire. It astonished him that people might think he was so powerful, and so heartless, that he could take another person's life. Okay, so maybe he'd taken a swing or two at opponents in the past. "But I haven't punched anybody in the face in the last couple years, let alone all this stuff."

The murders of both Biggie Smalls and

Tupac Shakur remained unsolved, but Puffy continued to grow increasingly exasperated with speculation that he'd been in any way responsible. Likewise, when *Time* magazine dared to ask him point-blank if Bad Boy had ever been affiliated with L.A. street gang the Crips, he balked at the suggestion. He was insulted at the mere idea he could behave so stupidly. "Why would I have a company worth over $200 million and jeopardize that by hiring security that does not have the license to carry firearms?"

When the rumors concerning gang involvement refused to die down, Kurt Loder offered Puffy another chance to clear the air. The Bad Boy CEO stressed that they'd never hired Crips, nor any gang faction, to serve as security. The company tried to conduct its business dealings like anyone else, but because Bad Boy was operated by young black people, the assumption was that it didn't follow the law.

In fact, on the night of Biggie's murder, the security team had included off-duty police officers. Just the same as Madonna, or Sylvester Stallone, or any big public figure in entertainment, Puffy and Biggie had traveled with bonded security men to protect them.

Yet Compton, California, police claimed they'd received conflicting information from gang informants. So could Puffy possibly have been unaware of wrongdoing at Bad Boy? Not as far as he was concerned: he scrutinized every detail of business at the label, so he didn't have to fear accepting responsibility for everything that went on there. He signed off on everything. No, Bad Boy had never employed gang members as security.

Puffy was also discouraged that hip-hop and rap were constantly the sole target of blame for violence of this nature. He felt that the problem permeated the entire community that his music had sprung from. Discussions had started only because two of the most important and best-loved figures in hip-hop were dead. And while the deaths of Tupac and Biggie had focused new attention on the matter, it wasn't going to abate even if their murders were solved. The violence and drugs and gangs didn't go away when the camera crews and reporters left. The killings and violence had to stop, and it had to be stopped because the community wanted it to. Something had to be done to help the families and friends dealing with such things every day.

As if he didn't have enough concerns to occupy his time, Puffy also had to address other rumors that came up from time to time about him. In light of the tremendous ups and downs of his life, it wasn't too shocking that some misguided souls still insisted that the ugly scar on his right wrist was the remnant of a suicide attempt—when instead he'd gotten the bizarre slash scar by mishandling a champagne glass.

Stranger still, whispers that Puffy batted from both sides of the plate—sleeping with men as well as women—grew louder when controversial radio DJ Wendy Williams of New York City's Hot 97 took it upon herself to post photos of Puffy on her Internet web site that she claimed were homoerotic. One of the pictures in question depicted Puffy and his protégé Mase leaning in very close to one another. Sure, they could possibly be about to lock lips, but the angle they're depicted at suggests they're probably just speaking very intimately, or trying to be heard over a loud commotion.

In England, where *puff* is slang for a man who is light in his loafers, the press brought the rumors up again. "I ain't that," he said with a chuckle in *The Face*. Besides, *puff* didn't have the same connotations in America. His name meant whatever he said it did.

When *Vibe*'s Sacha Jenkins asked him if there was any truth to the suggestions that he was gay, he said he couldn't even imagine why somebody would suspect that. He didn't bear any malice toward gays and lesbians, he wisely said, but he wasn't one of them. Besides, he noted, similar rumors had circulated about every black man who'd made it big, from Eddie Murphy to Mike Tyson to Russell Simmons.

\* \* \*

## The High Price of Success

And whether or not you loved and respected Puff Daddy, nobody could argue that he had not indeed "blown up" in stunning fashion. In June, he threw a magnificent Tyson vs. Holyfield party to celebrate the boxing match, and show the world that he was coming to grips with Biggie's death.

The fete was held at his East Hampton mansion on a cliff overlooking the waves, in a scene reminiscent to some of Andre Harrell's celebrated events of just a few years earlier. Security men in slick black suits moved discreetly among the crowd. Three enormous television screens showed the fight for the sports fans. An ice-cream truck distributed Popsicles, ice cream, and beach balls, and there was a full dessert buffet featuring apple and cherry pies, cookies, and chocolate cake. Guests relaxed in the hot tub, cavorted in the swimming pool, and mingled with friends and colleagues. Throughout the party, Puffy circulated among the crowd, smartly attired in a pink silk shirt, accented with a gold chain.

In July, Puffy launched another enterprise, his Caribbean restaurant in Manhattan, named Justin's. A smart, elegant establishment, it featured a tasteful, curving mahogany bar, a state-of-the-art sound system, and curtains Puffy himself picked out. He named the eatery after his son, Justin Dior Combs. The world might be singing the praises of "Puff," "Puffy," or "Puff

Daddy," but his son tended to be more direct. "He calls me daddy," Puffy told *The Face*.

As a proud father and a hip-hop kingpin, Puffy was frequently grilled on issues such as censorship and violence in rap. He claimed that he didn't object to hard-core records carrying parental warning stickers: kids didn't need to listen to certain albums until they were mentally mature enough to understand the full meaning of what they were hearing, and comprehend the gravity of the topics being discussed. Perhaps some truths were a little too severe or scary for tender young minds. He told *Time* that even though most raps were reality-based, and expressed vital viewpoints, perhaps they weren't pertinent to ten-year-olds.

As for Justin, he wasn't allowed to listen to Biggie's *Life After Death*. Nor, for that matter, were Biggie's children. When writer Sia Michel from *Spin* visited the set of a posthumous Notorious B.I.G. video shoot in April, she witnessed Puffy sprinting the length of a tour bus (in his Versace designer underwear) to flick off a track before four-year-old T'Yanna Wallace could overhear her departed daddy talking dirty.

There were even tracks on *No Way Out* Puffy didn't let Justin hear. "He just listens to the singles," he emphasized to Michel. "The cleaned-up singles."

Puffy had to be accountable for his actions, and to bring up Justin in a responsible fashion.

And that meant he had to treat the music he released with just as much care. This was why sending out positive vibes was the primary concern of his music.

But being a pop star and hit producer wasn't always a picnic, as Puff Daddy, Mase, and the Notorious B.I.G. elaborated on in "Mo Money Mo Problems," the second of Biggie's post-humous singles from *Life After Death* to reach the number-one slot on the pop charts. It was the only time in the history of contemporary pop that a deceased artist had enjoyed two number-one singles. Plus, it was the fourth chart-topping tune of '97 to feature Puff Daddy. Bad Boy now joined the ranks of Motown in the history books as the only other label to launch their first four number-one singles all in the same calendar year.

Puffy made little secret of the inspiration he'd taken from Motown and its founder, Berry Gordy. That was part of why he was forever teaming up artists in his musical family with one another, because it was a formula that had worked for Motown. "When the Supremes were hot, they did something with Marvin Gaye and Michael Jackson and the Jackson Five," he observed for *Billboard*.

Speaking of the Supremes' Diana Ross, "Mo Money Mo Problems" borrowed liberally from her 1980 smash "I'm Coming Out." That tune had been crafted by Nile Rodgers and Bernard Edwards of Chic, who had created "Good

Times" in 1979, later the rhythmic basis for an earlier crossover rap sensation, "Rapper's Delight," by Sugarhill Gang. Once again, Puffy's proviso that his hits were often bigger than those by the artists he sampled came true: "I'm Coming Out" had only gotten as high in the charts as number five.

The B.I.G. track had been composed at a point in Biggie's career when both he and Puffy felt like they couldn't avoid trouble unless they chose never to leave the house, which wasn't really an option. They loved making music and entertaining people, which meant being in the public eye. "So we wanted people to know we don't do this for the money, because the more money we see, the more problems we see."

The hits just kept on coming, too. "Mo Money Mo Problems" didn't stay at the top of the charts for long, but the next song to take its place was also a Puffy production: "Honey," by pop songbird Mariah Carey, hit the top spot on September 13. Puffy had held down the number-one slot *all summer long*.

An enormous hip-hop fan, Carey had contacted Combs and asked him to produce a few tracks for her latest album, *Butterfly*. It wasn't the first time the two had worked together. Back in 1995, she'd roped him in to remix her track "Fantasy," and the version he delivered, complete with a meatier bass line and a rap from Ol' Dirty Bastard of the Wu-Tang Clan, was the one most fans preferred. That single had also been a number-one hit for Mariah.

But during work on the *Butterfly* tracks, Puffy's insistence that every minute detail be flawless actually got in the way, so much so that he was barred from the recording studio when Carey was laying down her vocals. "I'm trying to work on that," he said. He was such a demanding perfectionist that sometimes he didn't give singers a chance to breathe properly: "I've been banned from a lot of studios." For "Honey," Mariah laid down the vocals over and over, until she felt she'd gotten it perfect. Then she handed all of them over to Puffy. He claimed there were over a hundred to choose from.

Mix engineer Michael Patterson concurred in *Vibe* that Puffy never stopped working until he felt a track was impeccably perfect. Puffy's production squad of Hitmen—including Nasheim Myrick, Deric "D-dot" Angelettie, Stevie J., and Ron "Amen-Ra" Lawrence—were all polished pros, but Puffy was the master.

"I know how Michael Jordan feels when he's on the court because that's the way I feel in the studio: like I'm the man," Puffy elaborated in a *No Way Out* press release. He didn't want to sound brash, but there was no other way to approach a task so important. "If you're trying to be the greatest you got to go into it

197

like you are the greatest." With one second left in a game, Michael Jordan wouldn't be hesitating, thinking, "I might make this" as he shoots. That's how Puffy treated recording. "I don't make a record like it *may* be a hit. It *is* a hit."

But in the studio, when Sean Combs was producing someone else, the larger-than-life Puff Daddy took a breather. He didn't act like a star if he was working with another artist. Like any other outstanding producer, he remembered that he was in their employ, and remained at their service. That required keeping his ego in check, and doing whatever it took to elicit the best performance possible from his subject . . . right down to making them tea, if necessary.

Besides, at heart he was a fan. How could he not get excited when he paused and realized the phenomenal talent in the room with him, be it Boyz II Men, R. Kelly, or Mariah Carey?

The magic worked once again for Puffy and Mariah. For the Bad Boy remix of "Honey," Puffy even brought in Mase and The Lox to add some raps. And in the action-packed video, Puffy and Mase got their cheeks pinched by Mariah, in a gesture that recalled moments from the crime epic *The Godfather*.

"That freaked them out," she said, laughing, in *Entertainment Weekly*. The boys took anything to do with gangster life a little more seriously than Mariah. But she appreciated that they seemed to know the secret to making people have a good time, too. That's why she'd wanted to work with Puffy again. "He's brought back fun party records," she observed in a later *EW* story. She saluted him for breaking down the barriers and making hip-hop palatable to mainstream audiences.

One key to Puffy's incredible success had been ample exposure on MTV and other music video outlets. It seemed impossible to turn on the television in 1997 without seeing him and his crew, regardless of who the featured artist in the video was. In particular, "I'll Be Missing You" had dominated TV airwaves. But in *Rolling Stone*'s year-end wrap-up, Puffy insisted the number of videos he appeared in had been greatly exaggerated. "I only been in a couple," he swore. "They've just been so big that everybody exaggerates." It was an exceptionally rare display of understatement from Puffy.

Puffy chose to pay MTV back for all their lavish attention with his performance at the MTV Music Video Awards on September 4. The day before, he played down the show he and the Bad Boy posse had planned in tribute to Biggie. He and Mase wanted people to look forward to the program as a giant celebration: they wanted to look out and see a sea of smiles, to bask in waves of positive energy. "We're most looking forward, as two young black brothers who've been on MTV, to seeing the races come together from hip-hop to rock and roll, from black to white to Chinese," he told reporters. He wanted the entire Radio City Music Hall audience to throw their hands in the air, and "wave 'em like you just don't care!"

Once again the ghost of Biggie seemed to hang in the air that Thursday night. When the Notorious B.I.G. snagged the Best Rap Video honors, Puffy brought Voletta Wallace and the whole Bad Boy crew up onstage to accept. (And when self-proclaimed Antichrist Marilyn Manson performed, the Bad Boy tables politely averted their eyes and turned away in a display of their Christian faith.) But the real homage came when Puff Daddy and Faith Evans came out to deliver their unstoppable "I'll Be Missing You."

Puffy and Faith were accompanied by a thirty-two-member gospel choir and backing vocalists on sliding platforms. Biggie's face shone down from a set of oversize video screens, and Puffy's own dancing was complemented by a clutch of nubile dancers. But the biggest surprise came with a hydraulic lift that hoisted up no less a guest star than the man who'd originally written and performed "Every Breath You Take."

"He wanted me to dance as well!" Sting was later quoted as saying in *Vox*. Wisely, the senior pop sensation declined to join Puffy in even the littlest box step. He felt confident the song would speak for itself.

As a testament to Biggie and to how far Puffy had come, the tremendous significance of pulling off such an ambitious production number at the MTV Music Video Awards wasn't lost on Puffy: the Bad Boy family had pulled out all the stops because it was a special occasion. Although he and Sting would work together again, this had been their first meeting. Puffy said the British singer had impressed him with his humility and manners. His positive karma had boded well for the performance, and what it represented. "He definitely blessed the whole situation," he told *Vox*.

The production number was a stunning piece of pop-music history. But it shouldn't have surprised anyone who'd been paying attention. Along with making hit records, making history seemed to be what Sean Combs—in all of his guises—did best.

# 14

## The Family Trip

In mid-October 1997, Puffy unveiled some
shocking but uplifting news for Notorious
B.I.G. fans: *Life After Death* would not be the
rapper's last album. Puffy planned to take
unreleased tracks from the Bad Boy vaults and
fashion them into the third album of Biggie's
unfinished trilogy. He revealed that there were
demos and other tracks of Biggie's that hadn't
been released.

The album would begin with early demos,
move through unreleased songs made during
his lifetime, and conclude with a couple of
numbers that had never been heard before.
Because Puffy had decided to take a historical
approach to the material, he described the
album he was compiling as a "documentary."
Voletta Wallace and Puffy would supply the
commentary that held the whole project
together. The record would be entitled *Born*

*Again* and was scheduled for an early 1998 release date.

Not that anyone was likely to forget Biggie Smalls anytime soon. In *People* magazine, Lil' Kim revealed that she had moved into his old town house and started every morning by kissing the box his cremated remains rested in. "When Biggie died, I thought I was going to be on drugs or commit suicide," she admitted in *People*. She wanted to give up, but when she communed with Biggie's spirit, she said he told her not to quit. And she hoped that no matter what tensions had existed between them in the past, she and Faith could bury the hatchet and admit they'd both loved, and had been loved by, Biggie.

Yet Puffy had even more startling news to share with fans that same week in October. Despite the tremendous sales of *No Way Out*, he didn't have any immediate plans for another Puff Daddy album. In fact, it was very likely this would be the first, last, and only full-length Puff Daddy release, he revealed on *MTV News*. He'd never planned on becoming a recording artist full-time. "At least on *No Way Out*, I had something I wanted to talk about." Unless he needed to address an issue as serious as Biggie's loss via music again, he couldn't see much point in making another Puff Daddy album. "I would probably just make them for other people."

# A FAMILY AFFAIR

* * *

At the beginning of November, Puffy climbed up one more rung on the steep ladder of success with the kickoff of the "No Way Out" tour. There hadn't been a hip-hop tour on such an ambitious scale in recent memory, and Puffy planned on giving people a show they'd never forget. For assistance, he handpicked artists he worked with as well as some personal favorites. And the lineup was stunning: Jay-Z, Busta Ryhmes, Usher, Nas, Foxy Brown, Lil' Kim, Mase, old-school DJ Kid Capri. And topping it all off was a headlining set from Puff Daddy and the Family.

Six of the artists involved had Top 10 singles at the time of the tour, yet they all carved time out of busy schedules to hit the road with Puff Daddy. Rapper Jay-Z noted that since "rap tours really don't get to go out," this was a tremendous opportunity for all the artists invited, and had generated ample excitement from the performers. Besides, he noted, if this tour went smoothly, similar outings might become annual events, and put outdated fears concerning live rap shows to rest.

As early as a month before the tour began, Puffy convened all the artists involved for production meetings held at Justin's. He wanted to "lay down the rules" for everyone, to make sure that they all knew what they were getting into, and appreciated the importance of living in family style for the six-week tour. Any animosity between acts from the past needed to be laid to rest. No guns or weapons of any sort were to be permitted on tour buses or in venues. Puffy wanted everyone on board to understand that if they could pull off this tour, all the performers involved stood to sell even more records. More important, they were taking hip-hop culture to a whole new level, reaching more fans than ever before.

Throughout a week of strenuous rehearsals in Albany, New York, Puffy put his acts through their paces. He wanted artists to hit their mark and move, make every gesture look like they meant it, and give the best show they possibly could. Every detail was carefully choreographed for maximum impact.

When the show opened in Albany, at the Pepsi Arena, on November 7, the hard work and planning paid off. The show was a state-of-the-art marvel, a special-effects spectacular. But it was the performers who really made it extraordinary. 112 offered up romantic ballads while displaying their sexy physiques. Usher went one step further and concluded his big hit "You Make Me Wanna . . ." by dropping his trousers to show off his skintight boxer briefs. Mase and The Lox exchanged dreams of how they'd spend their last day on earth in "24 Hrs. to Live." And Lil' Kim, the Queen Bee, strutted about in vibrantly colored skimpy ensembles, telling the men just how she expected them to service her needs.

Artists kept their sets short so the energy level never waned. The formula worked. "With its variety show pacing, the concert was designed as a capstone to one of the most remarkable five-year runs enjoyed by any performer-producer in pop history," wrote Greg Kot in the *Chicago Tribune*.

For Puff Daddy's set, he pulled out all the stops, strutting around a three-tiered stage. He had a mobile pulpit that swung out over the audience and brought out dancers to accentuate his own steps. There was a gospel choir and a eulogy for Biggie, who once again beamed down from three giant video screens. Puff and Lil' Kim went toe-to-toe with risqué rhymes, but Puffy made sure the crowd knew he meant no disrespect. "We're just having a little bit of fun," he told the fans. "We must respect each other."

And while there was a lot of talk about fat bankrolls and the Benjamins up onstage, Puffy stressed that he just wanted to give people what they wanted to see. He reminded MTV viewers that they weren't out there to make money; they wanted to brighten people's lives. "We came out here to go and touch everybody," he said. "We spent a lot of money on production and explosions, and flying through the sky and things like that so everybody could have a good time." Cheering crowds were all the payment Puffy needed.

December 1, the night of the New York City

show at Madison Square Garden, saw Puffy make good on a very special promise. Bad Boy Entertainment, Arista Records, and BMG Distribution had agreed to donate all the profits from "I'll Be Missing You" to the Christopher Wallace Trust Fund, set up in memory of the Notorious B.I.G. for the benefit of his two children, T'Yanna and Christopher, Jr. At a special press conference before the concert, Puff Daddy, along with Arista Records' Clive Davis, presented a check for $3 million to Voletta Wallace, who accepted the money on behalf of the children.

Puffy admitted in his presentation that 1997 had been a very hard year, but also a tremendously rewarding one. "One thing that life has taught me is that it's so important to make sure that you give back and to make sure that you try your best to constantly make changes with the things that you see that are wrong in the world."

But there was more money to be generously doled out that same evening. Puffy also donated a check for $100,000—a start-up sum drawn from his own producer's royalties— to the new Christopher Wallace Foundation. With Voletta Wallace serving as chairwoman, this organization would concentrate on the improvement of educational opportunities for young people.

And another check, in the amount of $200,000, was presented to Sister Souljah on behalf of Daddy's House Social Programs, the not-for-profit organization for underprivileged children that Puffy had founded and financed. Fifty cents from each ticket sold to the "No Way Out" tour shows was being donated to the Daddy's House charities.

That same night, there was a special ceremony onstage, too. Even as the music for Sister Sledge's disco classic "We Are Family" pumped through the sound system of Madison Square Garden, Puffy shouted out for them to cut the music. In front of the whole entourage, he announced that he had something very important he wanted to do. He turned and presented Mase with a platinum award for *Harlem World*, the young rapper's chart-topping debut Bad Boy album.

Mase turned right around and gave Puffy an even more impressive plaque, one that showed that *No Way Out* had now passed the quadruple-platinum sales mark, meaning over four million copies of the album had been sold. "Mine only got one," Mase complained in jest to Puffy. "You got four!"

With the "No Way Out" tour, Puff Daddy and the Family brought hip-hop to a wider audience than ever on the road. "People were cramped on each other, white and black people mixed up together," he shared with delight after a show in Detroit. Everybody was dancing, hugging, jumping around, regardless of class or color. And nobody had a problem with anybody else. It was all cool. Because they'd all been brought together by one thing: a profound love for hip-hop.

Puff Daddy and the Family crisscrossed the country, heading for the final date scheduled in Denver, Colorado, on December 22. In the meantime Puffy had yet another new hit single on his hands. Puffy and Sting teamed up once again for a remix of the old Police song "Roxanne," specially commissioned for inclusion on *The Very Best of Sting and the Police*.

The original version dated back to 1979. Puffy's new interpretation combined samples from the UTFO hip-hop classic "Roxanne, Roxanne." It was recorded at the Hit Factory, remixed at Daddy's House, and featured a guest rap from Pras of The Fugees. The single had debuted at number one on the *Billboard* Hot Dance Music Maxi-Singles Sales chart. More remarkably, Puffy's name and talent packed enough pull to get a New Wave song almost two decades old in the top five of the Hot Rap Singles chart. And the only things preventing it from climbing higher were Puff Daddy's own "It's All About the Benjamins" and Mase's "Feel So Good."

For his part, Sting said he hadn't asked Puffy to remix "Roxanne" as a commercial maneuver, but rather as an artistic move. By inviting Puffy and Pras to tinker with the Police original incorporating the rap and samples, they opened up Sting's song to a new audience, via an art form he admittedly knew next to nothing about. The mix was bursting with cultural reference points for Sting, who found it a bit odd to hear urban beats buoying up a vocal performance he'd made twenty years earlier, as a fresh-faced twenty-five-year-old. By his reckoning, Puffy's ability to combine the old and new yielded a completely new musical genre.

"The Police aren't on it," he said in *Vox*, "but what the hell!"

As 1997 drew to a close, seemingly every publication and media outlet in the country wanted to know Puffy's thoughts on the year. What did he see as the greatest breakthroughs in music? The tremendous diversity of artists who'd reached the upper echelons of mass success, from the techno-punk of Prodigy, to the squeaky-clean pop of Hanson and the Spice Girls. "These are all different styles of music that have been exposed this year, just different feelings and different vibes that just made the big musical gumbo that much more flavorful," he cheered for an MTV year-end wrap-up.

But it went without saying that the man who'd had the biggest hand in the greatest number of hits—as a performer, songwriter, remixer, or producer—was Puff Daddy himself. Which was why he told *Rolling Stone* his biggest achievement of the year was opening *Billboard* every week to see how many weeks he'd held the top slot for the rap, R&B, or pop charts, and keeping tabs on how many records he'd broken. *Rolling Stone* readers would vote him Artist of the Year.

"I wake up every morning and I feel blessed," he reiterated.

## No Slowing Down

Nineteen ninety-eight started with a bang for the Bad Boy family, with the release of *Money, Power and Respect*, the first album from The Lox. Their single "If You Think I'm Jiggy" had blown up at MTV, capitalizing on the exposure they'd already garnered via their raps on cuts with Puff Daddy, Mariah Carey, and others.

Although the talented trio had been affiliated with Mase for a spell, it was an older Puff Daddy alumnus who initially hooked them up with the Bad Boy stable: Mary J. Blige.

Sheek of The Lox told *MTV News* that Mary was their original number-one fan. "She was loving our music before anybody, and she just brought us to Puff." At the time Puffy was seeking a rap group to round out his artist roster. The two teams hit it off instantly. "It just clicked like that. It was chemistry."

The nominations for the National Academy of Recording Arts and Sciences' thirty-ninth annual Grammy Awards showed that the industry had taken notice of the landmark year Puff Daddy and the Bad Boy roster had enjoyed, nominating him for numerous awards, most notably the prestigious distinction of Best New Artist. But he also got nods in categories like Best R&B Song (for cowriting "Honey"), Best Rap Album (for both *No Way Out* and as producer of *Life After Death*), and Best Rap Performance by a Duo or Group (for three tracks: "Can't Nobody Hold Me Down," "I'll Be Missing You," and "Mo Money Mo Problems").

Nineteen ninety-seven may have been the year of Puff Daddy, but Sean "Puffy" Combs showed no signs of slowing down in 1998. That is, until his doctor ordered him to postpone a scheduled European tour that would have kicked off in January and continued throughout the spring. If Puff Daddy didn't let up the pace a little bit, exhaustion was going to take a dangerous toll; the dates overseas would have to be rescheduled.

No matter, for Puffy still had plenty of new projects to tend to on American soil. He spoke of launching a clothing line, Sean John, and a customized sneaker named the PD. Tony Thompson had signed to Bad Boy, and Puffy was still entertaining notions of completing a gospel album he'd been talking about throughout 1997. He wanted to write books and appear in movies. The FOX television network was talking about launching a variety series called *Puffy's House*, and Warner Bros. studios was courting him for a role in the motion picture *Lethal Weapon 4*. There was talk of a line of Justin's foods, and perhaps more restaurants.

And most important, Kim Porter, his girlfriend of four years, was pregnant with his second child, due in April.

From his humble origins in Harlem, Sean Combs had climbed to the top of the recording industry, surviving several tragedies that might have devastated lesser men, and those with weaker faith, along the way. Now fans and entertainment power brokers spoke of him in terms once reserved for the likes of Elvis Presley and The Beatles.

When *Vibe* brought up these comparisons, Puffy admitted they took his breath away. He had become a phenomenon on a previously unimaginable scale for a young black man. But the groundbreaking sales and popularity of Puff Daddy and the cadre of artists in his crew showed that racial barriers in popular music were finally dissolving once and for all. Puffy said that viewing things in terms of black and white wasn't as viable as it once had been. Prejudice might always be a problem, but its horrible grip had been loosened.

For all his achievements, his sole directive was still to accomplish all the things he and Biggie had planned on doing together. He wanted to focus on making Bad Boy the biggest and the best, and delivering records and performances that made the maximum number of fans a little bit happier.

Sean "Puffy" Combs, the superstar known to millions as Puff Daddy, didn't want to be remembered by history solely as a black music icon, he told *The New York Times*. There wouldn't be a label big enough to describe his successes. Puffy insisted that he and Bad Boy Entertainment wouldn't rest until they were as big, if not bigger, than Steven Spielberg or Twentieth Century-Fox. There was simply no other way. "I'm going to go down as a music maker that was so incredible that he represented all of culture."

# KEEPIN' IT REAL

*Post-MTV Reflections on Race,*
*Sex, and Politics*

## by Kevin Powell

Cutting-edge cultural critic Kevin Powell—journalist, award-winning poet, music-video producer and director, and all-round renaissance talent—drops the bomb on racism, sexism, hip-hop, and survival in his first collection of over-the-edge cultural commentary.

Powell takes us along on the dizzying tightrope walk that is life lived at the polar extremes of the hip-hop generation. Like the musical movement created by his contemporaries, KEEPIN' IT REAL samples the sights and sounds of American life and reshapes them in an honest, provocative soundtrack for our times—and the times ahead.

Published by One World/Ballantine Books.
Available in your local bookstore.

"Extraordinary. A brilliant, painful, important book."
—*The New York Times*

# THE AUTOBIOGRAPHY OF MALCOLM X

## As told to Alex Haley

If there was any one man who articulated the anger, the struggle, and the beliefs of African Americans in the 1960s, that man was Malcolm X. His autobiography is now an established classic of modern America, a book that expresses like no other the crucial truth about our times.

Published by Ballantine Books.
Available wherever books are sold.